Praise For

Women's Lives, Women's Legacies

Using a deft combination of biblical theory, feminist analysis, moving quotations, and personal experience, Rachael Freed has produced a work that is both inspiring and practical. Writing exercises throughout the book allow Freed to accompany her readers in absentia, urging us onward as we consider what our spiritual legacies might be, pointing our thinking as we begin to formulate commentary designed to make our deepest wishes known to those most important in our lives. This is a thoroughly successful mapping for anyone remotely interested in shaping the values of a lifetime into "gifts" for the future.

> – Toni A. H. McNaron, Distinguished Teaching Professor Emerita,
> University of Minnesota, and author of *I Dwell in Possibility: A Memoir*

Women's Lives, Women's Legacies is a significant and meaningful contribution to the literature on spiritual legacies. This book will instill confidence in anyone wishing to undertake the creation of her spiritual-ethical will.

> – Barry K. Baines, MD, cofounder of The Legacy Center and author
> of *Ethical Wills: Putting Your Values on Paper*

Women's lives are too rarely the stuff of history, and even less of legacy. Which is why Rachael Freed's work, *Women's Lives, Women's Legacies,* is so important. Freed gives us simple yet powerful tools to intentionally shape the inheritance we want to leave behind. She gives us a new rendering of history to reclaim the lineage and consequence of women's lives.

Like every good sub-version of history, women's legacies will initiate and gain power in our living rooms and kitchens, our community centers and places of worship – anywhere that women gather. I can't wait to be a part of it!

> – Bonnie Bazata, Center for Women's InterCultural Leadership, Saint
> Mary's College, Notre Dame, Indiana

I felt an urgent need to pass to my daughters not only my dreams for them and my values, but also the idea that these are the most important legacies I have. And it is crucial that this legacy be in writing, for writing is itself an act of faith.

— Wendy Schornstein Good, estate planning attorney and mother of two

A warm invitation to bequeath future generations with wisdom, love, devotion, and all that has mattered most in our lives. A priceless gift to women everywhere.

— Dona Billey-Weiler, certified Women's Legacies facilitator and chairperson for the Sage-ing Council of Spiritual Eldering, Michigan

This is a beautiful book with a soul. Rachael Freed has taken the concept of ethical wills and enhanced it, enlarged it, and made it accessible to women of all faiths. Her book is a tremendous legacy to others and provides a rich and most useful set of practical instructions for anyone who wants to pass on their values to future generations.

— Larry Raphael, senior rabbi at Sherith Israel, San Francisco, and former director of the Department of Adult Jewish Growth at the Union for Reform Judaism

Women's Lives, Women's Legacies is a shining contribution to individuals and institutions concerned with the matter of cultural continuity. It is a thoughtful, well-written, caring book, a delight to read, a delight to follow. In detail and in form, it is friendly and accessible. It possesses a kind of "god mother's" loving touch. In an intimate, lively, and learned way, Rachael Freed shows us how the use of a spiritual-ethical will may become the instrument of self-reflection and personal narrative.

You do not have to think of yourself as a writer in order to be fruitfully guided by her exercises and examples into fashioning a kind of testament to your life. But beware: by the time you are done, you may realize you are more of a writer than you thought.

— Peter Pitzele, author of *Scripture Windows* and founding member of the Institute for Contemporary Midrash

Women's Lives, Women's Legacies

Women's Lives, Women's Legacies

Passing Your Beliefs & Blessings to Future Generations

∼ *Creating Your Own Spiritual-Ethical Will*™

RACHAEL FREED

Fairview Press, Minneapolis

Published by Fairview Press, 2450 Riverside Avenue, Minneapolis, Minnesota 55454. Fairview Press is a division of Fairview Health Services, a community-focused health system affiliated with the University of Minnesota and providing a complete range of services, from the prevention of illness and injury to care for the most complex medical conditions. For a free current catalog of Fairview Press titles, please call toll-free 1-800-544-8207. Or visit our Web site at www.fairviewpress.org.

Library of Congress Cataloging-in-Publication Data
Freed, Rachael.
  Women's lives, women's legacies : passing your beliefs and blessings
to future generations : creating your own spiritual-ethical will /
Rachael Freed.
      p. cm.
Includes bibliographical references.
  ISBN 1-57749-119-X (trade paperback : alk. paper)
1. Wills, Ethical--Authorship. 2. Feminism--Religious
aspects--Judaism. 3. Genealogy--Religious aspects--Judaism. 4.
Self-perception--Religious aspects--Judaism. 5. Jewish women--Religious
life. I. Title.
  BJ1286.W6Z83 2003
  170'.82--dc21
                                              2003003704

First Printing: September 2003
Second Printing: May 2004
Printed in the United States of America
08 07 06   8 7 6 5 4 3

Cover by Laurie Ingram Design, www.laurieingramdesign.com
Cover image: Spain, Caceres, Olive Grove by Charlie Waite
Author photo by Shirlee Engebretson
Permissions and credits on pages x–xi

Fairview Press publications, including *Women's Lives, Women's Legacies,* do not necessarily reflect the philosophy of Fairview Health Services.

This book is dedicated to my grandmothers, Rosa Brodsky Friedman (Rachel) and Minnie Simon Bernstein (Mindel), whose legacies have profoundly inspired my life and this work. May their unique qualities enrich generations yet unborn.

Acknowledgments

The seeds for this book were sown and nurtured by many women over the years. Each of them has taught me something sacred by her writing both in and out of legacy circles, where students and teachers are peers. I am grateful for all that I have learned from them: to listen deeply; to respect and find joy in myself and all women, no matter what our differences; and to embrace the profound experience of belonging to a community of women across many generations. They have shared their souls and their writings, allowing me to see the blessings they've been to their loved ones, to future generations, and to our beloved planet. These women – some of whom are named here – have contributed to this book in many ways, and I offer my gratitude: Carolyn Abramson, Amber and Robin Anderson, Sandy B., Sandy Baines, Bonnie Barland, Beth Barron, Jane Bassuk, Jeanne Bearmon, Dona Billey-Weiler, Pamela Borgmann, Clara M. Bungert, Amy C., Rebecca C., Maureen Caron-Circele, Nancy Carter, Ethelyn Cohen, Patricia Cummings, Stephanie Czerniecke, Deborah Dora, Carol Ferris, Nicole Barchilon Frank, Bonnie Denmark Friedman, Cindy G., Melanie Gainsley, Dawn Gillette-Kircher, Felicia Gonzalez, Wendy Schornstein Good, Kay Grindland, Karen Johnson Gustafson, Judey H., Khoua H., Bev Harries, Gretchen Heath, Judy Hostnick, Wendy Jerome-Stern, Gale Kaplan, Joyce Kelley, Susan Deborah King, Barbara Levie, Christine Levin, Verna Lind, Nancy Lundborg, Bev Lutz, Janice Maxson, Jessica Miranti, Pat N., Elspeth Nairn, Barbara Ottinger, Marsha P., Jodi Patoka, Yvette Pennacchia, Helen Redman, Susan Richards, Karen Robertus-Schierman, Sara Rosen, Dana Rubin, Mary V. Schuster, Kathi Snead, Sister Agnes Soenneker, Josephine Stewart, Deborah Levin Stillman, Irene Stillman, Sophie Bea Stillman, Sandy Swirnoff, Marilu Thomas, Susan Eastman Tilsch, Mary O'Brien Tyrrell, Antoinette Williams, Julie M. Worwa, and Letitia Zilar.

Others whose lives, writing, and teaching have inspired me and my work include the Adath Jeshurun women's study group, Ilene Alexander, Barry K. Baines, Joan Borysenko, Julia Cameron, Joan Drury, Joseph Edelheit, Marian Wright Edelman, Ellen Frankel, Laura Geller, Natalie Goldberg, Eva Hoffman, Andrea London, Toni McNaron, Sara Lynn Newberger, Tamar Ghidalia Ostfield, Julie Parker, Debbie Perlman, Peter Pitzele, Judith Plaskow, Larry Raphael, Anne Roiphe, Abby Seixas, and Michael Steinlauf. Thank you.

I am also grateful to my publisher, Lane Stiles, who saw the promise in this work and has never stopped believing in it. And last, this book would not be what it is without Stephanie Billecke, my editor. Thank you for your commitment and elegant refinement of the book's ideas and design.

Thank you to the individuals and publishers who have generously given permission to use the following copyrighted works: "Lot's Wife," page 17, by Constance H. Gemson, previously published in *Four Centuries of Jewish Women's Spirituality* © Ellen M. Umansky and Dianne Ashton, eds. (Beacon Press, 1992). Excerpt, pages 20–21, from *Generation without Memory* © Anne Roiphe (Simon and Schuster, 1981). Excerpt, page 25, © Carol Ferris. Excerpt, page 27, © Verna Lind. Poem, page 30, from chapter 1, "Voices of the Mothers," appearing on page 5 of *The Voice of Sarah* by Tamar Frankiel, copyright © 1990 by Tamar Frankiel, reprinted by permission of HarperCollins Publishers Inc. My writings about Gramma Minnie, pages 40–42, adapted from an article that originally appeared in *Minnesota Genealogical Journal,* vol. 30, no. 3, 1999. "Rose," pages 44–45, © Marilu Thomas. "Legacy from My Single Aunts," pages 48–49, © Gretchen Heath. "My children . . . ," page 52, © Karen Johnson Gustafson. "An Old Story," page 75, © Gale Kaplan. "My Mother's Song," page 91, by Patti Tana, first appeared in *Ask the Dreamer Where Night Begins* © Patti Tana (Kendall/Hunt Publishing, 1986). "Marking Him," pages

100–101, © Margaret Hasse, appeared in *Touched by Adoption*, edited by Nancy A. Robinson (Green River Press, 1999), and *33 Minnesota Poets,* edited by Monica and Emelio DeGrazia (Nodin Press, 2000). "A Theology of Motherhood," page 103, © Karen Johnson Gustafson. "No Kissing," page 108, © Beverly A. Lutz. "I thought blonde women knew," page 112, © Nancy Lundborg. Excerpt, page 124, © Nicole Barchilon Frank. Excerpt, page 127, © Janice Maxson. Poetry excerpt, page 131, adapted from "I Hope I Don't Trip," © Ethelyn Cohen. Poetry excerpt, page 133, from "Grace Cathedral," © Eve Hearst. "The Death of Jacob," page 181, © Ruth F. Brin, appeared in *Harvest: Collected Poems and Prayers,* Second Edition, by Ruth F. Brin (Holy Cow! Press, 1999). Excerpt, page 183, © Pamela R. Borgmann. Excerpt, pages 186–187, © Sandra Butler and Barbara Rosenblum, appeared in *Cancer in Two Voices,* by Sandra Butler and Barbara Rosenblum (Spinsters Ink, 1991). "Post Humus," page 190, © Patti Tana, originally appeared in *Ask the Dreamer Where Night Begins,* by Patti Tana (Kendall/Hunt 1986). "To My Daughters: Exhortation to Prohibit Mourning on Cessation of the Motion of My Blood," pages 194–195, © the estate of Ella Berniece Bixler. United Nations Environmental Sabbath Prayer, page 204, appeared in *Earth Prayers from around the World* © Elizabeth Roberts and Elias Amidon, editors (HarperSanFrancisco, 1991), reprinted with permission of Elizabeth Roberts. Excerpt, pages 205–206, © Kathi Snead. "Grandma Bertha Davis," pages 208–209, © Sandy Swirnoff. Letter, page 232, © Milton Lieberman. An exhaustive effort has been made to locate all rights holders and to obtain reprint permissions. If any required acknowledgments have been omitted, or any rights overlooked, it is unintentional. If notified, the publishers will be pleased to rectify any omission in future editions.

Contents

Introduction

> There is no greater gift we can give ourselves than the understanding and healing that comes with this type of writing. Just as an employment resumé provides a snapshot of one's work history and skills, a spiritual-ethical will gives your loved ones and family a picture of your soul, a portrait of who you really are.
>
> – Kathi Snead

Legacies are the footprints we leave behind after we die. They prove that we were here: we lived, we mattered, we made a difference. Sometimes we leave tangible legacies like children, artwork, crafts, poetry, heirlooms, or gardens. Other legacies are financial, including endowments, charitable donations, even corporations. But most legacies are the fruits of a life well lived. They're found in every tree we've saved by buying recycled paper, every friend we've cheered with our jokes and laughter, and every stranger to whom we've shown kindness.

Women's contributions to the world, whether large or small, are always significant. But unless you document the meaning of your unique legacy, one day your stories and values will be lost forever, buried in the dust of history. By putting your values into words, you not only preserve your legacy, but offer a special gift to loved ones: your spiritual-ethical will.

A spiritual-ethical will is not a legal will, which documents how your estate should be distributed after you die. It is a record of who you are – a gift to the present and to the future, one that can be offered to loved ones while you're still alive. Your spiritual-ethical will is an opportunity to articulate your values, impart your wisdom, bless your loved

We must not, in trying to think about how we can make a big difference, ignore the small daily differences we can make, which, over time, add up to big differences that we often cannot foresee.

– Marian Wright Edelman

ones, and express how you hope to be memorialized after your death. One day your descendants will hold this document in their hands and know who you were, how you lived, and what you contributed to the world. This may be the most important writing you will ever do.

Legacy work is different from autobiography, memoir, life review, and genealogy not so much in what is written, but in our intent. We write to preserve our personal, familial, and communal histories. We write to express who we are and what we value, to mark our place in the world, to be witnessed by others, to build community, to be remembered. We write to bless those who come after us with our love and wisdom. If our lives are to have lasting meaning, we must use them as a sacred link, consciously connecting the past and the future. We do this by articulating our legacies to those we love.

I have facilitated many legacy circles in recent years, helping women create their spiritual-ethical wills. These women represent all races, ethnicities, faith traditions, educational levels, and life situations. I've worked with homemakers and professionals; new mothers and grandmothers; women who are single, married, committed, divorced, and widowed. I've worked with immigrant women, abused women, incarcerated women, and women in all manner of personal transition, including those confronting retirement, divorce, grief, illness, and death. Few of these women were writers and many lacked confidence in their ability to express themselves, especially in writing. Some of their work appears throughout this book.

HISTORY OF THE ETHICAL WILL

The ethical will originated in Genesis 47–49, when Jacob called his twelve sons – but not his daughter – to his deathbed. Shortly before he died, he blessed his sons and extracted a promise that they would bury his remains in the land of Canaan, where his ancestors were buried.

Wisdom comes not by accumulation of more and more experiences but through discerning pattern in the deeper mystery of what is already there.

– Mary Catherine Bateson

By the twelfth century in North Africa and western Europe, the ethical will had taken the form of a written letter, a device used by fathers to impart ethical and religious instruction to sons. The letter also specified the children's responsibilities related to burying and mourning their father.

The ethical will remains, in many ways, a Jewish patriarchal tradition. Indeed, it is one reason that the Jews, historically a nomadic people, have survived for centuries. By celebrating their history, recounting their story, remembering their dead, and imparting the culture's wisdom to their children, the Jewish people have managed to maintain traditional values and connect future generations to the past.

It is painful, however, to note the near absence of women's participation in the ethical will tradition. In 1690, one woman, Glückel of Hameln, subverted cultural expectations by writing about her life and family history so that her children would know where they came from. At a time when the written word was the prerogative of men, it must have been a lonely, courageous act to write about subjects that moved women. And yet, legacy writing seems a natural undertaking for many women today. We are the weavers, the storytellers, the memory vessels who gather, build, and sustain our communities. Regardless of our religious beliefs, the ethical will is a powerful tool for unleashing our voices, power, and purpose.

At this precarious moment in history, we realize that life is fragile and we do not control the number of our days. Many of us feel a sense of urgency, a need to document our legacies and raise our voices to help shape this unfolding new world. We have an obligation to record our personal values and family stories. In so doing, we strengthen the fabric of civilization.

Set these words, which I command you this day, upon your heart. Teach them faithfully to your children.
– Deut. 6:7

My parents' example and messages keep me grounded when I am tempted to lose sight of what is important amidst the mounting demands of work and family and a culture that values things and style and packaging and publicity over substance and service and concrete action.
– Marian Wright Edelman

ABOUT THIS BOOK

I have renamed the ethical will to differentiate it from the patriarchal model and to define it more fully. Reflecting and writing about our deepest values is courageous, spiritual work; therefore, our goal is to write a spiritual-ethical will. And because legacy writing is a spiritual act, I have made reference to God throughout this book. Whether you use the name God, Goddess, Allah, Christ, Atman, Life Force, Creative Source, Higher Power, Higher Self, Divine Presence, Creator of the Universe, or some other name, I hope that you will not be offended by the names I have used. Allow your work to resonate with your own sense of the sacred.

The book is divided into three sections. In part 1, The Past, you will examine your family history and claim the legacies of your feminine ancestors. You'll also become acquainted with Sarah of Genesis, a recurring figure throughout this book. All women, no matter what their religious beliefs, will hear echoes of Sarah in their own lives. But for women who feel disconnected from their family roots — because of adoption, separation, abuse, family secrets, slavery, or lost records — Sarah can serve as an early ancestor, providing a much-needed sense of rootedness and belonging.

Part 2, The Present, addresses widely diverse components of who you are today, touching on work, play, motherhood, sexuality, spirituality, and more. These chapters are about self-discovery: before you can document your legacy, you must first know who you are and where you came from. The exercises here offer a firm foundation to prepare you for writing your spiritual-ethical will.

In part 3, The Future, you will begin putting your legacy into words, writing down your values, blessings, and wisdom for those you love. In addition, you will consider how you'd like to be memorialized after you die and how you want your money and other valuables to be distributed. In the last chapter, you'll decide which of your writings to

All theology is autobiography. As we tell our own stories, we often discover the divinity that is present in our lives.

— Rabbi Laura Geller

Tradition is not just what we inherit from the past; it is also what we create and pass on to the future.

— Marcia Falk

include in your spiritual-ethical will. This chapter will also guide you in editing and preserving your document and presenting it to loved ones.

Each chapter in this book offers an opportunity to reflect and write on a number of topics. The exercises are designed to help you find your voice and overcome any fears you may have about the writing process. Later you will transform these writings into a spiritual-ethical will, but for now you will write for yourself, from the heart. This work is not for your high school English teacher of old; there's no need to concern yourself with grammar, punctuation, or sentence structure. Simply write as if you were speaking and focus on your thoughts and feelings, noting sights, sounds, smells, tastes, and textures.

Use this book in a manner that feels right to you. You may wish to proceed in a linear fashion, one page at a time. You might read an entire chapter or section and do the writing later. You may skip certain sections, perhaps jumping to the chapters that feel most relevant. You might even read through the whole book, foregoing the exercises, and instead write a one-page legacy letter to each of your loved ones.

However you decide to use this book, please keep the following points in mind:

Store all your writings in one place. You may wish to purchase a three-ring binder to hold your work. Look for a beautiful binder with dividers, and label each section to correspond with the chapters in this book. Once you begin your legacy writing, you may feel inspired to go back and forth between sections, adding new information.

Prepare your sacred writing space. It's a good idea to set up a special place for your legacy work. Make your space beautiful and comfortable. You may want to have fresh flowers and green plants, a favorite piece of art, and a lovely view. If possible, make it a space for you alone and use it only for writing and reflection. This way you will draw energy to the place where you write, making it sacred to you. The more often you write there, the more power you will experience.

We should write because writing brings clarity and passion to the act of living....We should write because writing is good for the soul.
– Julia Cameron

Each time you return to the space and sit in your chair, you will feel energized and inspired.

Think of your writing as a spiritual endeavor. Perhaps you want to attract the energy of qualities you value for this work: serenity, clarity, honesty, courage. You may feel these qualities in a favorite painting, photograph, rock, shell, wall hanging, statue, or icon. Some women draw inspiration from music, candles, or incense. You might prefer to write by the light of early morning or in the quiet of evening.

Many women like to write at a typewriter or computer; others write longhand, using their favorite pen and lovely writing paper. Whatever you choose, be sure to file your writings in your binder when you are finished.

Gather your thoughts before each exercise. Set aside a time to write when you know you'll be free from distraction. Turn off the telephone, if you have to, and inform your family that you are not to be disturbed. You might prepare yourself with a hot shower or bubble bath to clear your mind. Change into fresh, comfortable clothing; maybe set out a beautiful china cup and begin steeping your favorite tea, or ready your mug and brew your special coffee.

You may want to begin each reflection and writing session with a short meditation or prayer. Remind yourself of the sacredness of your life and ask for divine guidance before you proceed.

Follow only the instructions that feel right to you. As you read each exercise, remember this Twelve Step slogan: Take what you like and leave the rest. There is no one right way to write; there is only your way. Some suggestions and examples will be helpful to you. Others will not. Take only those ideas that help you discover and express yourself.

Silence your inner critic. For many women, the very thought of writing feels threatening or evokes a sense of inadequacy. Try to remember that you are writing for yourself. Your writing doesn't have

The spirit needs constant care and nourishment, just like the body.
— Marianne Williamson

It is important for them to know that I did not make this thing up. It is rooted in a long and rich tradition that is theirs, and in this way they are blessed.
— Wendy Schornstein Good

to be perfect; you're simply giving yourself the gift of your own voice. As Lao Tzu said, "A journey of 10,000 miles begins with one step."

A blank page can be daunting to the most seasoned writers, so if you're not sure how to get started, try writing a letter. Pick up your pen and at the top of your paper write "Dear _____, today I am writing to you about _____." Use this technique whenever you're feeling stuck or struggling for the right words.

Write now, edit later. In chapters 1 through 11, you will write your most private thoughts and feelings. You will write only for yourself, clarifying and articulating your values, beliefs, stories, hopes, and dreams. Don't even think about editing at this time. Not all of your writings will end up in your spiritual-ethical will. In chapter 12, you will review your work and determine which writings to include in your legacy. Only then will you begin to edit and polish your document.

Experiment with different writing techniques, but don't lose sight of your goal. As you go through the chapters, you'll be introduced to a variety of writing techniques. After you've given each a try, you may decide that you prefer some more than others. You might also experiment with poetry, storytelling, stream of consciousness, and other techniques. Use the forms that feel right to you, but remember, your primary purpose is to mine your memories, thoughts, and feelings so you can communicate who you are and what you value. Don't let any writing style overshadow your reasons for writing.

Use the time suggestions to plan your daily writing sessions. Let yourself write at a comfortable pace, and take as many days as you need to complete each exercise. In a few cases, time limits will help you pace yourself as you work through emotionally provocative topics.

Repeat exercises as often as you wish. There is no reason why you can't write on the same subject more than once. Repetition may offer deeper insight to your thoughts and memories, ultimately enhancing

I believe we come into life as writers. We are born with a gift for language, and it comes to us within months as we begin to name our world. Words give us power.

– Julia Cameron

self-understanding. While the reflections and writings are arranged to build on one another, you are free to go back to earlier writings at any time. A later reflection may remind you of something you've omitted, or you may wish to expand on an earlier topic.

After each writing session, record your experience. Jot down a few notes about the writing process and how you feel about what you wrote. Keep these notes as a record of your feelings throughout your journey.

Date each writing. As you continue your legacy work, you will want to review your writings from time to time to see how you've progressed. Dates will allow you to put your work in context.

Keep your materials in a safe place. Your legacy work is private and sacred. Be sure to keep your writings in a place where no one will read them. When the time comes, you will determine which of your writings you want to share with others.

Get into the habit of writing. Writing regularly will help you maintain your momentum and shape the schedule of your project. The more often you write, the easier it will be to tap into memories and ideas relevant to your legacy work.

THE LEGACY CIRCLE

I recommend that women do legacy work in community whenever possible, preferably forming a sacred circle of four to twelve women. Women who work in legacy circles enrich their own spiritual journeys by witnessing the unique paths of others. As women share their writings in the circle, they come to appreciate their differences as well as their similarities. Celebrating uniqueness while rejoicing in the connection with other women changes the quality and depth of one's writing, infusing it with love and creativity.

If you choose to work alone, it's important to find someone you can trust who is willing to witness your writing and support your

What if there were no such thing as a writer? What if everyone simply wrote?
– Julia Cameron

What women need is the opportunity and the validation to name and describe the truths of our lives.
– Adrienne Rich

legacy work. You might also imagine yourself surrounded by a "virtual" circle of women. Some of these women have shared their writings in this book; many others have created and communicated their legacies but are not specifically represented in the pages that follow. If ever you need extra support in your legacy work, you may tap into this virtual community at www.womenslegacies.com. There you will find an Interactive Connections page where women across the country discuss their writings, ask questions, and share the joys and frustrations of creating a spiritual-ethical will.

If you choose to form a legacy circle, you may be tempted to invite your most intimate friends, but consider including women of diverse ages, ethnic groups, and educational backgrounds. Each woman will bring her own perspective to the circle; the more varied the views, the richer your experience and the more amazing the bonds among you will be. Together you will find your unique voices, your sense of belonging, your connection with the Divine. You will witness each other's joys, disappointments, secrets, and successes, and you will imprint the future with your communal experience and wisdom.

At your first meeting, welcome each woman to the circle. You might note that the circle is a place where all women are respected for their uniqueness. Everything said or heard in the circle is confidential, and it's important that every participant agrees to this at the start. The legacy circle is not an opportunity for literary discussion or criticism – for that you may want a writers' group. It is not for analyzing behavioral patterns or helping each other make decisions – for that you may want a therapy or support group. This is a sacred legacy circle, an opportunity for each woman to have her writing, life, and legacy witnessed by others.

Know that each of us is one thread in the tapestry of womankind, connected with all women across time and space, yet brimming with unique gifts, stories, experiences, and wishes for the future. In this

And the challenge to keep growing and changing even while forging an identity, to stay true to the present moment even while nurturing a sense of continuity with the past and the future – is that not the core of authentic living?
– Marcia Falk

spirit, you may invite each woman in your circle to introduce herself by saying one thing ordinary and one thing extraordinary about herself. The ordinary could range from "I don't floss every day" to "I am a mom." The extraordinary might include "I survived thirty-five years of secondary teaching," "I will die in this prison without holding my granddaughter," or "I am optimistic about the future of the planet."

Proceed to the first writing exercise, adhering to the designated time limit. Afterward, each participant may take the opportunity to read her writing aloud, though every woman has the right to pass. No participant should ever be pressured to share her writing. When a woman does choose to share, consider it a sacred gift. Set aside your judgments and any habits you may have of caretaking or "fixing" others, and listen with your full attention and respect. In so doing, you will increase the safety and holiness of the circle. Remember, a legacy circle is meant to support women in discovering and expressing who they are and encourage them in their commitment to document their legacies. What to write and read is always an individual's choice; safety and privacy must be the highest priorities.

In the presence of compassionate non-judgmental listening, miracles happen.
– Marianne Williamson

After everyone who wants to has shared her writing, you might go around the circle to comment on any surprises, difficulties, and insights you experienced during the writing process. Then, introduce the topic for the next meeting. All participants are encouraged to write at their own pace. Share your writings the next time your legacy circle comes together, and agree to meet regularly until each woman has completed her spiritual-ethical will.

In *The Age of Homespun*, Laurel Thatcher Ulrich writes that, years ago, "[t]he revolutions of the spinning wheel and the thwack of the loom sustained the rugged virtues of hard work, neighborliness, and unaffected piety." Similarly, the documenting of our beliefs and blessings will sustain the souls of our loved ones – and the human community – for many generations.

We stand together at the genesis of a sacred journey. While our ultimate aim is to create a spiritual-ethical will, our preliminary goal is to explore legacies we've received from the past.

Each of us yearns for a sense of belonging to family, ancestors, history. We will explore these connections in the chapters that follow, beginning with the legacies given to us at birth: our names. We will then identify the legacies left by our feminine ancestors, gifts not only of genetics, but of wisdom and life experience. Along the way, we'll enjoy the company of women who have traveled this path before us, drawing strength from their ideas, impressions, feelings, and words.

As you travel the past, you will collect a number of writing tools that will serve you on your journey. These techniques will help you engage in your explorations so you can mine the content of your history without undue concern about your writing skills.

Before we can give our stories, values, and wisdom to the future, we must first gather our legacies from the past. We now turn to family, ancestors, and the beginning of recorded history.

May you be refreshed and restored by your sacred journey.

PART ONE

The Past ~

CHAPTER ONE

What's in a Name?

You've heard people say, "I know it as well as I know my own name." But how well do you know your name? Most of us take our name for granted, never fully exploring this essential part of our identity.

Your name connects you to your family and ethnic group, to your heritage. It marks the place in the world where you belong. If you were named to honor an ancestor, historical figure, or literary character, your name connects you to the past. It speaks of memory, legacy, and immortality, of a special relationship with the person for whom you were named.

Consider how this baby will carry our American history: A woman giving birth on September 11, 2001, asked her rabbi to find the name of a victim of the terrorist attacks, so that she could name her baby after a person who was lost on that day. All the victims of 9/11 had names, and each is being remembered and mourned in a variety of ways. Here a woman chose to merge her religious naming tradition with the larger loss of our nation and the world.

Knowing the history of your name deepens your understanding of who you are. Your name follows you, conferring a sense of identity and belonging. Your name can shape who you become, and you, paradoxically, can shape your name, adding depth and meaning to your life.

Remember "Sticks and stones can break my bones, but names will never hurt me"? Not so! Childhood names and nicknames may remind you of old hurts endured on the schoolyard. On the other hand, you may fondly recall an affectionate nickname given by a person who loved you in a special way.

As adults, we continue to be sensitive about our names. Use of either a formal or intimate name is a powerful clue indicating what is expected of us in a given situation. We may feel surprised, even invaded, when a store clerk calls us by our first name as she returns our credit card. We may feel offended when our name is forgotten or mispronounced by someone we've met more than once, or when we're mistakenly called by the wrong name.

Women often struggle with names that diminish them, names that make them feel small, unimportant, even impotent. Many women prefer to be called by their full name, like Jennifer or Judith. They long to be free of Jenny or Judy, names they carried as girls.

If you think that names don't matter, look at the curiosity piqued over nameless women. Remember Lot's wife, one of the no-name women in Genesis? She turned around while fleeing the destruction of Sodom and Gomorrah and was turned into a pillar of salt. Four thousand years later, modern poets, novelists, theologians, and others continue to be fascinated with Lot's wife. By writing about her they hope to glean some understanding of who she was – her legacy to the world – without the cues and clues to be found in a name.

Lot's Wife

Her name is nameless,
known as his wife, wearing his title,
draped by desire.

To be Lot's wife was her mission
By lot, by chance, by error,
she followed him with conviction, a sleep-walker weaving in a dream.

Then she is asked to leave this land
where there was fire she tamed and food she grew.
Her calling is to forget.

He hurries her to pack for the family, to leave this old land,
place her thin memories in a bundle she will not need them.

The future waits vast but violent.
The new colors are vivid and burn her eyes.
The sun is harsh in its power.

She wants to hold the past, ripe as first fruit.
For this she looks back to remember,
and slowly turns to salt.

– Constance H. Gemson

Family Names

When a baby is born we ask, "What did you name it?" We name babies not only to acknowledge their uniqueness, but to "brand" them with a family affiliation and endow them with a sense of belonging. Our name is the beginning of a deep connection to our history. It is the first legacy we receive from our family, tribe, and culture. It may even influence who we will become.

In most Western cultures, a name binds a baby to her father's family. Think about common family names: Sally Johnson (Sally, son of John), Dora Davidson (Dora, son of David), Susan Richardson (Susan, son of Richard). In Iceland, women carry the suffix dóttir, or daughter, attached to their father's name, as in Erica Bjornsdóttir.

Play with this idea. How might a man feel about carrying his mother's name, perhaps George Marysdaughter (George, daughter of Mary) or Sam Debrasdaughter (Sam, daughter of Debra)?

Each of us can connect with her matriarchs as well as her patriarchs. Here is my name identified with my maternal ancestors:

I am Rachael, daughter of Beatrice (Beyla).

I am Rachael, granddaughter of Minnie (Mindel) and Rosa (Rachel).

I am Rachael, great-granddaughter of Eve (Chava), Carolina (Chaya), Bessie (Beyla), and Deborah Ida (Debra Chaya).

REFLECTION AND WRITING *(10 to 30 minutes)*

Write your name in connection with your feminine ancestors. Some women are able to trace their maternal lineage back through many generations; others will find their histories complicated by slavery, adoption, immigration, assimilation, or poor record keeping. Go back as far as you can. You may want to take some time to contact relatives and check family Bibles or other records.

When you are finished, read your list of ancestors aloud into a mirror, if you are working alone. If you are working with other women, share your names with your legacy circle. As your names are heard, you may feel a profound connection with your female ancestors. And you will enjoy witnessing others as they have a similar experience.

Next, reflect on what you felt as you did this exercise. Did you experience history unfolding, a sense of connection, power? Write some notes to record your observations.

Power and Identity

Naming is an act of power. I recall my two-year-old grandson, Mitch, marching around the house and pointing at everything that caught his eye. "Name," he demanded, and we told him the name of each object. He was on a serious mission, replacing confusion and helplessness with certainty, order, and control.

The beginning of wisdom is to call things by their rightful names.
– Chinese proverb

We see this in the Harry Potter series as well. Hesitant to ask Dumbledore about Voldemort, Harry stutters and calls him You-Know-Who. Dumbledore responds, as any wise wizard would, "Call him Voldemort, Harry. Always use the proper name for things. Fear of a name increases fear of the thing itself."

Like any powerful tool, the act of naming has been abused throughout history. In the sixteenth century, Spanish explorer Hernando de Soto replaced the "pagan" names of native peoples with Christian names, depriving descendants of their heritage. Until the end of the 1940s, Native American children were separated from their families and tribal traditions, placed in boarding schools to be "civilized," and forced to accept Christian names. In the twentieth century, the Nazis systematically stripped Jews of their names and tattooed numbers on their arms in an effort to dehumanize them and obliterate their

My mother, the youngest of five, was playing under the kitchen table — the year must have been 1914. Her aunts, her father's sisters, were preparing dinner. In the midst of their conversation they spoke the family name. The name they had used in Poland. The name that had been changed to Phillips some time after their appearance before the immigration officer at Ellis Island. There was a sound of a toy rolling across the floor. They dragged her out. Raging and weeping and calling to God in a steady stream of Yiddish, they jumped on her. One aunt pinched the child's arm until the child too was crying. One of the aunts shouted, "If you ever tell anyone the name you heard, your children and your children's children will be cursed with disease and pain, misfortune and early death. If you tell this secret to any of your older sisters or brothers, their children too will die in agony. Not a soul must know the name of our family before we came to America." The aunts allowed the little child to make her escape and returned to the cutting and the peeling and the chopping — the preparations for a meal that my still frightened mother was unable to share.

My mother told me that story when I was a child. "Tell me the name," I begged her. "I won't tell anyone," I promised.

"No," she said, "I can't."

I asked my uncles and my aunts and they said they didn't know of any other name. (Perhaps the family had always been called Phillips or Phillipovska.) "Who cares," they said. "Forget about it," they cautioned.

In 1962 when my mother was dying and she knew she was dying, although everyone was promising her health and long life, I sat at the edge of her bed. My baby daughter was playing with her grandmother's jewelry box; strings of pearls, gold bracelets, charms and earrings were rolling about the carpet.

"Please," I said, "now tell me the real family name. If you don't tell me perhaps no one will ever know."

"I can't," she answered, and it was a great effort for her to talk. "I don't want to curse you or the baby."

"You don't believe that," I said. "That's superstition, primitive, childish, magic-ghetto whisperings." I had recently finished college and I thought I knew fact from fiction.

"No," she insisted, "I would bring down the curse on you and your children."

I felt an ancient shadow in the room, a creeping darkness that contained more than just approaching death. Curiosity was stronger than fear.

"Please," I said, "write it out on a piece of paper."

She turned her head away from me and closed her eyes.

Imps and demons of the ghetto, Lilith and Samuel were cheated that day. Phillips was the family name and the family history started at Ellis Island. Lately I have been wondering if not knowing the real name was not a form of curse too. What was the family shame? What was the terrible secret? Was it nothing more than being Jewish and foreign? Or was it perhaps some criminal act that had been committed on the distant ground and covered by a hasty flight to the New World, across an ocean that forgave the old sins in anticipation of the new? Was it perhaps some paranoid belief that the czar's army could reach over the waves and recall its deserters, its impressed servants, and reclaim lives that had been thought free? Or was this wiping out of the name simply an expression of eagerness to become American, to undo the greenhorn condition, to forget what humiliations had been and enter a new world, with a clean slate, where one need not follow in one's father's footsteps and one might redeem the promises of a somewhat silent and unbending Deity?

– from *Generation without Memory,* by Anne Roiphe

Help me to name myself,

Name Maker,

Recapturing the purity of soul

Your Finger placed within me

As I sighed my first earth

breath....

– Debbie Perlman

history. And for centuries, slaveholders in the United States and Europe branded slaves with their own names, expressing ownership while simultaneously severing family and historical connections.

Yet the power of naming has also been used to invoke freedom and renewal. It allows us to resist oppression, reclaim our heritage, or forge a new identity. By casting off slave names, Malcolm X and many others made a powerful statement highlighting the loss of history that accompanies the loss of names. Cassius Clay (Muhammed Ali) and Cat Stevens (Yusef Islam) both embraced Islamic names to celebrate their new identity as devout Muslims. And throughout history, countless immigrants have discarded their "foreign" family names in order to better assimilate into a new culture – a decision that subsequent generations would often regret in their yearning to reconnect with their history.

All over the world, names are believed to bring protection from evil or power over death. In *The Binding Chair,* Kathryn Harrison writes of pregnant women in China: "In excitement and confidence they consulted with diviners, they bestowed grand and propitious names on their unborn children to guard them against harm and evil spirits. . . ." In many cultures, it is an age-old custom to change the name of a person who is sick. Coo, a Laotian immigrant, wrote that she and her twin sister, Ka, became seriously ill when they were babies. Their father called in a shaman for help. Unable to save her sister, the shaman changed Coo's name to Khoua, a male name, so that death would not know where to find her.

A name change also signifies a rite of passage, expressing purpose, mission, even a new identity. In Native American cultures, tribal elders may give a young person a new name as she leaves on a vision quest. Or, when a young person discovers her spirit guide while alone in the wilderness, the spirit may reveal her true vocation and real name.

Name changes have been used to mark significant life transitions or transformations since the beginning of recorded history. In Genesis

17:15–16, God told Abraham, "As for your wife Sarai, you shall not call her Sarai, but her name shall be Sarah. I will bless her; indeed, I will give you a son by her. I will bless her so that she shall give rise to nations; rulers of peoples shall issue from her." Any life transition may be marked by a name change. An inmate at a women's prison, for example, vows to change her name after she is released in order to have a fresh start. She believes her name is well known from her public trial, and she will never be able to live a private, normal life carrying that name.

A young rabbi recalls her visit with Rose, a hospitalized five-year-old who was miraculously recovering from a life-threatening illness and surgery. When the rabbi greeted the child by name, the girl corrected her, explaining that she now had a new name: Lily. When the rabbi later spoke with the child's parents in the hospital waiting room, she praised their wisdom in honoring their daughter's recovery with a new name. The parents looked at the rabbi in surprise. They thought it had been the rabbi's idea to change their daughter's name. But it was Lily who was wise enough to mark this transition from illness to health.

Women who choose to bind themselves to a life partner, whether through marriage or a formal commitment ceremony, often contemplate changing their last name. Some women are eager to drop their surname to attach themselves to a new family, a new role. Others want to keep their name because they feel that it best represents who they are. Many women struggle to find a middle ground, using their family name as their new middle name, or hyphenating the two surnames in order to bind themselves to both their father's family and their partner's family. Some women will use their partner's name in their personal life, reserving their family name for their professional life. And some couples agree to give up their family names and choose an entirely new name to mark their relationship.

What's in a name?
That which we call a rose
by any other name would
smell as sweet.
– William Shakespeare

Wrestling with a name change often signifies a deeper conflict related to a woman's identity. Divorced women, for example, will often reclaim their family name, and with it a sense of safety or belonging. Some women choose an entirely new name to suit their post-marriage life, a symbol of renewal and individuality. One woman, who came to her legacy circle wearing a different hat at each meeting, took the first name of a beloved grandmother as her last name when she divorced. The name meant even more to her when she found out that her grandmother ran a millinery shop.

At birth I was named Rhoda Jean Friedman. When I married, I never considered keeping my maiden name. But, having no brothers, I was aware that my father's family name, Friedman, would be lost. So, I dropped Jean and took the initial *F* to perpetuate his name, becoming Rhoda F. Levin. When I later separated from my husband, I had just become a grandmother. I sensed that a new life was beginning for me, and I was in many ways reborn. One way to express this transition was to acquire a new name.

For my first name I decided to use Rachael, my Hebrew name, which also was my grandmother Rosa's Hebrew name. It seemed appropriate to drop my husband's surname. As I searched for the right last name, I took another good look at Friedman and finally came to a decision. It felt a little strange and a lot courageous to drop the *m-a-n* off the end, but at my age, the idea of writing "man" over and over again seemed a waste of precious time. To prevent mispronunciation – I could hear it at my favorite breakfast place: "two eggs fried, over easy" – I changed the spelling. I chose *A* for a middle initial, and I have fun telling friends that it stands for "Almost." My new name, Rachael A. Freed, reverberates deeply and feels like the new me.

Now that you have read about names and how they relate to power and identity, I invite you to explore your own name.

Names embody the very specific and potent essence of an individual; through its name, which contains its form and nature, every creature derives vitality.
– Simkha Weintraub

I was nearing forty, and my only child, Matt, was packing to leave for Georgetown University. I had been a single parent for most of his life, and his leaving was difficult for me. Since friends had dissuaded me from taking a job in D.C. (dissuading was putting it politely: "NO" they said when I broached it), I was facing a future that would bear no relationship to the past.

I thought: I should change my name. It was the right time to find the name that really belonged to me.

I thought: I'll take back my maiden name. "That's your father's name," said Matt's grandmother. "And besides, you need to keep your name because it's Matt's last name."

I thought: I'll take a stage name. (Since my married name was Wood and since I worked in the timber industry, I had suffered years of cracks like: "Gee, it's a good thing you don't work in pork bellies.") My secretary had nicknamed me Lil (short for Leadfoot Lily, something about my driving habits), so I thought, perhaps Carol Lily or Carol Lilly might be a good name to take.

The first child in my family, I was named Carol Ann. I was from the beginning deeply in love with and loved by my grandmother, Ferris Gherke Leuschel. When my younger sister was born, she was named Christine Ferris. But throughout my childhood, my mother would look at me and sigh, "I should have named you Carol Ferris."

The day my son boarded the plane for D.C., I drove to Oregon's coast at the invitation of Byron Ferris, a man whom I had met briefly in the course of business. "You'll be very well chaperoned," he said, which I was. It didn't stop us from falling in love, and, one week later, the day I turned forty, he proposed and I accepted.

"Can I take your name?" I asked him, to which he replied, "You can call yourself anything you want."

Byron Ferris and I married and I had my name.

– Carol Ferris

REFLECTION AND WRITING   *(30 minutes)*

Your name is an essential part of your legacy. Without your name, how could you be known, be remembered, leave a part of yourself for the future? You may find that delving into your name is unexpectedly empowering. It allows you to strengthen your roots, connect with your heritage, and recognize your name – your identity – as a unique strand in the human tapestry.

To stimulate your thinking about your name, reflect for no more than ten minutes on the questions below. Then, at the top of a fresh sheet of paper, write "My dear (daughter, niece, friend), today I am writing to you about my name."

Let yourself write for twenty minutes. If you have more to say about names, repeat this exercise as often as you need to until you are ready to move on to the next chapter. Enjoy yourself! Consider some or all of the following:

- How did you receive your name? Are you named for another person, real or fictional? Do you or did you have a special relationship with that person? How has that person's name influenced your life?

- How important is your name? How do you imagine you would be remembered without your name? What does your name mean in your family? Historically? Symbolically?

- In what ways has your name protected you or endangered you? How has it been a burden, a difficulty, or a blessing? Has your name made you feel powerful? Powerless? How does your name affect your sense of purpose?

- Has your name ever changed? If so, why? How did you feel about your old name? How has your attitude toward your name changed at different times in your life? Have you ever had nicknames? How do you feel about them?

- Does your name feel right to you? Have you ever considered changing your name?

- Have you named another person? What was it like – awesome, difficult, fun, interesting, meaningful, solemn? Or was it something you never thought much about?

I was a wanted first born. If I was to be a girl, I was to be named for Vernon and Irene Castle, the most dynamic and beloved ballroom dancers of the '20s and '30s. My parents adored them. The evening before I was born, they went to a movie featuring the Castles. Lovingly, I was named Verna Irene.

Always I have been proud of my name. It is unique. There are not a lot of Vernas to be confused with. But it is a daunting name to live up to. I have spent my life growing into my name. I have wanted Verna to be associated with compassion, leadership, humor, adventure, friendship, discipline, acceptance of diversity, and, above all, Jewishness.

During my early teen years, my name changed to Vernie. My girlfriends and I were going through the typical identity search. We all wore the same uniform: Levi's jeans, long-sleeved shirts with sleeves rolled up, loafers, and bobby socks. We decided one day to give ourselves new names. I was named Vernie. I liked it. Friends from those years still call me Vernie.

During high school, Vernie stuck. Even my mother called me Vernie. When she called me Verna it meant I was in trouble. My father called me Verna.

A favorite high-school dance teacher, Marion Weiser, had wanted me to attend Mills College, which had a wonderful dance major. Verna wanted to attend. She knew it would open her life to innumerable possibilities. Vernie was afraid to go. She was afraid to be far from home and to compete in a world of wealthy girls. She knew she had the talent for dance, but she was unsure of her academic ability.

Vernie won. She went to the University of Colorado to become Verna. My ballerina days were over. Verna switched to modern dance, which has been the love of my life to this day.

—Verna Irene Holtzman Schwartz Lind

- If you have children, what would you tell them about their first, middle, or last name? What would you tell them about your name?
- Some people use special names known only to their communities. How are names used in your ethnic or cultural group?
- Consider writing a story about family names that you want to remember and pass on. What do you want others to know about these names?
- If you have never thought about names before, consider writing about names as they relate to personal, family, political, historical, cultural, literary, and spiritual contexts.

When you are finished writing about names, put your writing into your binder for safekeeping. We will refer to it again in the final section of this book.

CHAPTER TWO

$\mathcal{D}$iscovering Sarah

In this country, where most of us are the issue of immigrants, many people have no connection with their roots. Our grandparents and those before them, intent on assimilation, often traded their heritage for a chance at a new life. The more they succeeded, the more they lost touch with the past. Stories were lost or watered down as our ancestors mingled with people of diverse cultures.

Today, even with family trees and sophisticated genealogical tools, many of us remain empty-hearted. We yearn for meaningful connection to a past that will provide us with a history, with stability, with a sense of belonging. We ache for stories that might round out our lives and fill a void we can hardly define.

Before we explore our personal family stories and histories, we'll first examine the archetypal Western family: Sarah and Abraham. Connection to that family is within every woman's grasp, whether or not she considers herself religious. Sarah's life – her story – resonates with our own.

Sarah,
noblewoman,
why did you leave your homeland
to become his princess, Sarai?
What did you know,
what did you see ahead,
you who saw the destiny of our people?
Iscah,
prophetess,
you saw us before you,
your daughters,
lost in a land yet farther away.
Speak to us from Machpelah,
comfort us in our struggles,
laugh with us
that we may share the joy
of the impossible.

– from *The Voice of Sarah,* by Tamar Frankiel

The Story of Sarah

According to the Judeo-Christian-Islamic tradition, Sarah was a wife of Abraham, the patriarch of nations. From a secular perspective, she is a fundamental figure in Western literature and perhaps the earliest recorded female immigrant in Western culture. By knowing her, we may increase our sense of belonging to the human family and to our gender.

When we meet her, her name is Sarai. Her story is but briefly mentioned in the Bible, sketched only as part of her husband Abram's story (Gen. 12–25). What we know about her comes from the perspective of the men who recorded this story from the oral tradition. Their purpose in telling it was to document nation building and establish Abraham as the founder of the people Israel.

Sarah's story is as powerful today as it was 3500 years ago, because she and her family struggled with life issues similar to our own. Unlike the Greek gods and goddesses, the characters of Genesis are truly human. Their strengths and limitations, their frustrations and suffering, mirror our own.

Who among us has not had to leave home and family to become herself, to journey into her future? Who among us doesn't fear the unknown? Who has not grieved the loss of family, the disappointment of lost dreams?

Who has not found beauty and femininity to be dangerous? Who has not known betrayal? And if a woman discovers she is infertile, how powerful is her effort to have a child any way she can?

And how common is it to struggle with the challenges inherent in blended families, including feelings of frustration, anger, pride, and shame? Or to love a child with such strength that we'd do anything to protect that child and his or her future? Yet, who can say that she's never abandoned her child or her friend? Who has not felt powerless,

Patriarchy has denied Sarah her story, the opportunity for freedom and blessing.
– Phyllis Trible

Our ancestors and our ancestral wisdom live in our blood and in our bones.
– Julia Cameron

To be rooted is perhaps the most important and least recognized need of the human soul.
– Simone Weil

or abused the power she had? Who has not failed in her faith in God or tried to control destiny?

And so it was with Sarai, the archetypal pioneer, beautiful woman, manipulator, ferocious mother, betrayer, and betrayed.

REFLECTION AND WRITING

In this exercise you have an opportunity to give Sarah the voice she was not given in Genesis. In other words, you will write through and for Sarah, sharing her hard-won wisdom and leaving a message for her loved ones. We begin with her life story.

Sarai is a beautiful priestess and the wife of Abram, who leaves his father's house with all his household and goes forth to a land promised him by God. Because droughts and famine are common in this desert land, Sarai and Abram travel from Canaan to Egypt for food. Fearing that he will be killed for his beautiful wife, Abram asks Sarai to pretend she is his sister. Pharaoh finds Sarai beautiful and takes her into his palace as a wife, and all goes well for Abram. When God responds with plagues, Pharaoh confronts Abram with his lie, returns Sarai to him, and sends them off with gifts. One of these gifts is a servant girl, Hagar.

Following subsequent years of barrenness, Sarai suggests that Abram take Hagar to bear them a son. Sarai's plan is to raise the son as her own. Hagar agrees, but once she conceives, the close relationship between the two women changes: Hagar is disrespectful to Sarai; Sarai is harsh with Hagar. Ishmael is born.

When Sarai is ninety, God changes their names to Sarah and Abraham, a sign that she will be blessed with a son as part of God's covenant with Abraham (Gen. 17:6). Overhearing God's dialogue with Abram, Sarai laughs at the thought of having sexual relations with her one-hundred-year-old husband and bearing a child at her age. When God questions her, she becomes afraid and denies that she laughed. Isaac, which means "he laughs," is born.

Sarah, fearing Ishmael will get the legacy she hopes for Isaac, demands that Abraham cast Hagar and Ishmael out of their camp. Abraham complies, sending them into the desert.

Sarah is not mentioned in the next part of the story, where God tests Abraham by asking him to sacrifice his beloved Isaac. Her inexplicable death at age 127 and her burial in a cave in Machpelah, near Hebron, are noted in Genesis 23:1–2. Interpreters suggest that Sarah died when she discovered that her son was all but slaughtered.

~ *Part 1* *(20 minutes)*

If you are working in a legacy circle, have someone read the following directions aloud, slowly and clearly. If you are working alone, you might have someone read you the directions, or you might record them yourself, pausing after each instruction.

Imagine that you are traveling back to Genesis, to Sarah's desert home at the time just prior to her death. Give her a moment to appear to you. Notice everything you can about her. Get a sense of her physical being. Be aware of her strengths, limitations, and the qualities that make her who she is, both ordinary and extraordinary. Consider how current events of the time define her life struggles and life lessons. Reflect on what she is proud of, what she is ashamed of. Notice her successes and disappointments. Who or what does she fear, and how does she respond to her fear? Whom does she love and who loves her?

Take a moment to imagine yourself in her tent in the desert, in her very being. Become her. Knowing that you have had a long life and that death will come soon, you experience some urgency to share what you've learned and communicate to those who will live after you have died.

Now, Sarah, write your legacy in the form of a letter. You may choose to write to your child, Isaac; your stepson, Ishmael; your friend Hagar; your husband, Abraham, future generations, God, or any mix of these. Your letter might include your struggles and satisfactions, your regrets and fears, your loves and joys, your ethics and values – all that mattered most to you in your long life.

You may find that strong emotions and tears, hers and yours, accompany this writing. Continue to write, and keep breathing deeply.

Hagar, I don't know where you are or what your life is like now, but I feel an affinity toward you I have not felt before and I need to tell you before I die. We are sisters of a different sort – through the generation that comes after us. Both of us have a son whose fate is, and has been, decided by a man we have shared. I wish I could talk to you and say I'm sorry for not honoring your pain and heart. Forgive me for my jealousy.

Dear Ishmael, I ask you to forgive me for sending you away into the desert with Hagar. Many nights I cried as the desert sun followed you and left me cold. When you were born, I rejoiced in you, knowing that I could not conceive on my own. Hagar bore you, and I loved you as my own son.

Even though it broke my heart to send you away, the seeds of betrayal grew like poison in my heart. I claimed Isaac's birthright and denied you my love.

I continue to love you as the boy who filled my heart with joy. I am saddened not to know you as a man, yet comforted knowing you are really God's son. Forgive me. Love, Sarah

Hagar, I am deeply ashamed and neither could have known nor even imagined the consequences of my act. I didn't let myself think about it at the time. I didn't consider your future or Ishmael's, only my own and Isaac's.

I pray that I have not brought a curse on Isaac, or, for that matter, his brother, Ishmael. – Sarah

Dear Hagar: Our friendship has sustained me, how dreary my days will be without you. And yet, our devotion is nothing when compared to my love for my son and the future of the nation of Abraham. From me must come the seed for the future. God has granted me this great gift. I must ensure that it is not wasted. – Sarah

Dear God –

At this moment, just before my death, I realize how headstrong and willful I've been, taking destiny into my own hands, not trusting that you would keep your promise to Abraham. I didn't have to help you.

I pray that you will forgive me, and that I have not done harm to the future. I used Hagar for my purposes, and when she and Ishmael got in my way, I neglected their safety and well-being.

I am truly sorry and have no way to undo what I have done. Please forgive me.   – Sarah

Dear God,

It has been a long and hard life that you gave me. I never felt cared for by my husband. I was lonely in my barrenness.

It saddens me to die without feeling connected to you or being seen and appreciated by you. Women are also made in your image.

So I depart as I lived – lonely, deprived of connection to you, and saddened because of it.   – Sarah

God, I come to you angry, angry that I was not able or allowed to know you and your plans for me and my spouse. I'm angry because I hurt another woman, more than once, angry because I almost was owned by another man. I'm angry because I hurt a child.

I'm angry because without you in my life, I made my own life without your guidance. I made bad choices, choices I would not have made if I had been allowed to know you.   – Sarah

When you are finished writing, set aside your materials and, with your eyes open or closed, focus on your breath. Breathe deeply and slowly. As you do, return through time and space from Sarah's desert tent to the twenty-first century, to your special writing place, to yourself.

If you are writing as part of a group, take time to share Sarah's letter with the other women in your legacy circle. Like all of us, Sarah needs others to witness her life. Witnessing other women's Sarahs will broaden your perspective, open your eyes to the multifaceted interpretations of experience, and raise your appreciation for the uniqueness of each woman's perceptions.

You may decide to repeat this exercise, writing to another person in Sarah's life. Doing an exercise more than once can give you greater insight, enhancing your connection to your memories, thoughts, and values.

∼ *Part 2* (20 to 30 minutes)

Now, review what you've written. Take notes on what you thought and felt while writing as Sarah.

- What was ordinary and extraordinary about Sarah's life, feelings, actions, decisions? How was she unique, and how is she connected to all women? To you? What feelings, thoughts, conflicts, or issues do you share with Sarah? What was it like to connect with another woman, whether real or fictional, from another time?

- Natalie Goldberg, author of *Writing Down the Bones,* asserts that "writing is a physical act." How did it feel to write from the perspective of Sarah?

- What did you learn about yourself while writing as Sarah? Record any realizations you had. Which themes in Sarah's life spoke to you? Which of Sarah's relationships touched you? How?

- Reflect on your experiences as an emigrant – one who journeys from the known to the unknown, as Sarah did. Would you consider changing your name to mark or celebrate a significant transition?

When you are finished writing your letters and notes, put them into your binder. We will come back to Sarah in later sections of the book as themes of her life echo themes of our own.

~

Sarah thanks you for giving her a voice. What you have written in her name, from your own imagination, adds to a long tradition called midrash, which means "exploration" or "investigation." Since biblical times, midrash has been used to understand Scripture more fully and to help us see the relevance of sacred texts in our lives today. Madeleine L'Engle, a deeply committed Christian writer perhaps best known for her stories for young people, explains that "a midrash is a commentary on Scripture that attempts to fill in [missing] details but does not change the story."

Our purpose for doing this exercise was twofold. First, Sarah provides a universal sense of connection, one we can rely on even if we don't have access to a family tree or ancestral stories. As we put ourselves in Sarah's sandals we feel connected to a woman who struggled as we do, though her circumstances and life may at first have seemed very distant and unlike our own. In this exercise, we took a significant step toward interconnectedness, the awareness that each of us is unique, yet part of a larger, older chain of life.

The other reason for this exercise was to get us past our resistance to writing. Most of us don't think of ourselves as writers; in fact, many women fear that the act of writing will expose their incompetence. However, when women are invited to write for someone else, someone who had no opportunity to voice her values, ideas, pain, or love, they are able to pick up their pens, glad to help another woman.

Sarah would say thank you, sister, for voicing what I didn't have the opportunity to say or write before my death. I say congratulations

Midrash liberates the spirit encased in the text.
– Peter Pitzele

Narrative not only confirms human existence; it is the core of human culture.
– Jack Kugelmass and Jonathan Boyarin

Let us pray that all living beings realize that they are all brothers and sisters, all nourished from the same source of life.
– Thich Nhat Hanh

All acts of memory are to some extent imaginative.

– Eva Hoffman

The discovery of women in our history can feed the impulse to create midrash; midrash can seize on history and make it religiously meaningful.

– Judith Plaskow

for having written, and for getting through that old resistance. As you document your journey throughout this book, continue to set aside your expectations about how and what you should write.

This exercise is proof that you will be able to write your own spiritual-ethical will. The rest of the book is designed to help you discover and express what matters most in your life so you can celebrate it and communicate it to the future.

Though your cultural and ethnic background may be different from Sarah's, experiencing her life, values, and legacy may feel spiritually healing. You may now be deeply engaged with her – and with women's common history throughout time. Perhaps, after giving Sarah a voice, you realize that you are blessed with the right, the privilege, and the responsibility to express the value and meaning of your life. You may want to document where this legacy came from when you write your own spiritual-ethical will.

*May the roots of your
family tree grow deep
and strong.*

CHAPTER THREE

Your Family History

Each of us is one stitch in a richly textured family tapestry. Our histories link us with generations past, just as our legacies will link us with generations to be. This is why we seek out family stories, knowing intuitively that our roots – and therefore our legacies – are entwined with those of our ancestors.

But what if you have no stories? What if your family history wasn't handed down through the generations? What if your ancestors were stripped of their ethnic, national, religious, and family identities, either by choice or circumstance? What if you are the elder in your family, and there's no one left to identify those regal-looking, buxom, or deeply wrinkled women in your family album?

All is not lost. You have your intuition, your imagination, your ability to think. And in chapter 2 you became an experienced writer of midrash, a technique you will use to explore your family history. The practice of writing midrash emerged at the beginning of the first century C.E. Today it has seen a rebirth among women who struggle to recapture their heritage and the sacredness of their lives.

Women's stories are sacred, yet they are rarely expressed. To know who we are, we must first know where we came from. We need to discover the legacies that make up our family histories. One way to do this is to document the lives of our feminine ancestors. To illustrate this process, I introduce you to Gramma Minnie.

I knew little of my grandmother, who died in the summer of 1961. She and my mother had been estranged, and I saw Gramma on only a handful of occasions. My mother described her as vain, depressed, and dysfunctional, an image I carried in my heart until I began my search for the real Gramma Minnie.

It all started when my favorite uncle, the patriarch of the family, shared with me the following: after emigrating alone in 1898 at the age of eighteen, Gramma returned with her first infant daughter to her family home in Sanok, Poland, then traveled back to the United States.

Now, how and why would a vain, depressed, dysfunctional young woman travel alone with an infant from Illinois to Poland and back again at the turn of the century? What lessons am I to learn from this mystery, one hundred years later? What is her legacy to me?

First, I listed all the facts I knew about Gramma Minnie. Following threads from family records and using the local library, I uncovered the following:

1. Minnie was born in 1880 in Sanok, 110 miles southeast of Krakow.

2. Now part of Poland, Sanok was then part of Franz Josef's Austro-Hungarian Empire.

3. Minnie's father, Jacob Wolf Simon, was a cantor, chanting and leading daily prayers. Her grandfather was a Torah scribe, a holy profession requiring devotion, study, and humility. (A scribe writes the Torah by hand using a quill, parchment, and handmade ink. That work continues unchanged to this day.)

4. Minnie's mother, Chaya (Jacob's second wife), was so pious that she did not speak on the Sabbath until she was twenty-eight.

5. Minnie emigrated alone in 1898 to live with her half-brother, Max Simon, in Kenosha, Wisconsin. She was eighteen.

6. She married Eugene Bernstein, a Romanian, on May 3, 1902, in Kenosha, Wisconsin. They then moved to Elgin, Illinois.

7. She gave birth to six live children: Reva (1903), Lillian (1905), Isabelle (1906), Adolph (1908), Morris (1911), and Beatrice, my mother (1915). There are no extant records of miscarriages or stillborn children.

8. When her firstborn was an infant, she returned with the baby to Sanok.

9. Her second daughter, Lillian, died in the flu epidemic of 1918.

10. Widowed after twenty-eight years of marriage, Minnie lived another thirty years. She died on June 13, 1961.

11. Minnie was buried in the Lubavitch section of the Waldheim Cemetery in Forest Park, near Chicago. Her husband is buried in the Romanian section of the same cemetery.

It wasn't much, but it was a start. Now I needed to get a sense of who Minnie was and what life must have been like for her.

I'd read that Sanok, Poland, was in the foothills. But the foothills of what? Though it was nearing 9:00 P.M., I called the public library info line and was promptly transferred to the history department. A pleasant voice asked if she could help me. I told her what I wanted to know, and she directed me to hold.

When she returned to the phone, she explained, casually, "Sanok is in the foothills of the Carpathian Mountains."

The Carpathians! Oh my God, I thought, those are real mountains. Gramma Minnie's Sanok foothills soared several hundred feet as I heard the name, making me almost dizzy. This traveling she'd undertaken was intense.

The more we know about our families, the more we know about ourselves, and the more freedom we have to determine how we want to live.

— Monica McGoldrick

History is a card table of illusions, and we must sort through and pick the ones we wish to believe.

— Helen Fremont

I couldn't hold such a majestic piece of knowledge alone. I wanted the librarian to share the awe I felt. I thought of a related question, one that I was pretty sure I already knew the answer to, and matched her dispassionate tone with my own. "Am I correct that that's about 110 miles southeast of Krakow?"

She replied, after what I assumed was a glance at the map in front of her, "As the crow flies." As the crow flies! She was looking at an aerial view, she explained, but the distance between Krakow and Sanok was farther on foot. She saw no direct road, and the foothills were numerous.

All thoughts of a direct and easy route melted away, and I imagined my gramma's journey a hundred years ago, perhaps before railway access. I could almost hear the creaking wagon wheels and the panting of tired mules as they inched along the narrow way, which surely had no guardrails.

Breathless with excitement, I thanked the librarian for her help and we said good night. I remained sitting in front of my laptop, illuminated by a halogen lamp, surrounded by appliances and accouterments that would have bewildered Gramma Minnie.

The respect that began to dawn on me grew as big as I imagined the Carpathian Mountains to be. This woman, my grandmother, had gone alone with a baby through the Carpathian Mountains to get home. I needed to rewrite my account of Gramma Minnie to accommodate her power and courage and determination. My new perspective shifted everything.

I returned to my list of facts and added five words to the first line. It now reads: Minnie was born in 1880 in Sanok, *a small Carpathian Mountain village,* 110 miles southeast of Krakow. And this was just the beginning. In my search for Gramma Minnie I would delve deeper into each fact on my list. I would recreate Minnie in my mind as I clarified the unknown, filled in the gaps, and made sense of the contradictions.

Now it's your turn.

REFLECTION AND WRITING

~ *Part 1*   *(15 to 60 minutes)*

Choose one woman from your family, perhaps your grandmother, your great-grandmother, or your great-aunt. Pick a woman who fascinates you, or choose someone to whom you feel a strong connection. Write down all her names.

Next, create your list of facts. Number each fact and write everything you know about your relative. Your list may be very short or very long. It may take you three minutes or an hour.

When you have finished, review your list. What images do you have of places, times, stories, and details you've taken for granted? Do you see any gaps – contradictions or unanswered questions – in your information? In the next step you will begin to fill these gaps with details as grand as the Carpathians or as tiny as the date on a marriage license.

~ *Part 2*   *(60 to 90 minutes)*

List all your family members and anyone else still living who knows something about your relative. Here's where the modern conveniences of phone, fax, and email will come in handy. Plan to ask the people on your list for memories and stories that will flesh out your image of your ancestor and her life. Even if she seems unfamiliar, one-dimensional, or far away, you may be amazed at what you will discover.

Consider hunting down photographs, letters, recipes, and other tangibles that might be stored in someone's attic or basement. Remember, women's lives are often written in strange places: at the front of cookbooks and alongside often-used recipes; in songs, lullabies, rites, and rituals; and among superstitions passed down from one generation to the next.

Write down other resources that might help your investigation, including census records; birth, marriage, and death certificates; and genealogical books and Web sites. You might also look for books or articles about your ethnic or cultural history, which sometimes trace families and clans. At the very least they will paint a portrait of the place, circumstances, and time in which your ancestor lived.

Rose

I never wanted to be like my mother. It was my motto in life – "not like Mom." Most everything I did was calculated to not resemble anything she had ever done.

My mother was a second-generation Polish Catholic from Buffalo, New York. In the sixties she joined forces with the feminists, went to college, and became a sculptor. She announced, one afternoon, that she was resigning as mother and would only answer to her first name, Rose. Soon, Rose started smoking, cussing, and hanging around with other artists. I was ten years old and not very appreciative of the struggles of the housewife-sculptor life when homework was confusing or dinner was cereal. For the next ten years or so I endured avant-garde gallery openings, discussions on starving-artist angst, and lewd sculpture adorning our yard (to the chagrin of our middle-class suburban neighbors).

I went to college, got an impressive job, married, and joined suburbia. Then came the quicksand of my own midlife identity crisis, complete with spiritual malady. To know who I was, I had to find out who this woman Rose was in greater detail. I had become the antithesis of my mother, throwing the proverbial baby out with the bathwater. What had I missed in the bargain?

On a fact-finding mission, I took my mother to the Guggenheim Museum in New York City. My assignment was to listen to her without judgment, criticism, self-pity, or blame. I would see her as a person, not as my mother.

Before we even got to the second level, I was astonished at her knowledge of art, artists, and the chronology of theory. From across the room she could name the artist, year, and medium of each piece. Finally, as we faced an immense white canvas, I asked her, with some condescension, why it was art. It was white. It looked blank to me. "Use your eyes," she admonished me, causing me to shrink like a little girl. "From left to right there is a great change in the white. In small increments the artist has shifted the color to show his own shifts in perspective. By the far end of the painting on the right side, the color has transformed, and so has the artist. He is describing his spiritual experience."

I felt as if the cave of my soul would implode. My mother was a spiritual woman? God had blessed me with a spiritual mentor, the one source that I had negated! No wonder I was spiritually deplete. I could relate to the incremental understanding of spiritual truths she described – I had just seen it happen on the third floor of the Guggenheim.

My mother and I have reconciled in many ways since that day, as I have listened for more gifts from our mutual spiritual scavenger hunt. We aren't best friends yet, but I have more information on who I am and where I come from. Oddly enough, right when I got used to Rose, she decided that she preferred Mom.

– Marilu Thomas

Prioritize this list according to your interest and intent to pursue each option. Note those resources that you can begin researching immediately and those that may take more time and planning. Your goal is to gather detailed information about your ancestor in order to receive her legacy.

Though you might accomplish your goals in a week or two, you may find yourself updating this information – and your point of view – for years to come. Take notes on your experience. Document changes in your perspective as you proceed. Write about the feelings that accompany your discoveries.

When I began my search for Gramma Minnie, I felt like a diamond hunter in a coal mine. Here are some of the treasures I found:

- Minnie spent much time brushing her hair, and she kept a barrel of rainwater for shampooing.
- Because of her vanity, her family nicknamed her "Queen Marie of Romania" (a woman she greatly admired).
- She read several newspapers daily and was fluent in five languages.
- Although her husband worked for a fruit and produce company, she maintained her own herb and vegetable garden.
- She baked challa every Friday, and her oldest grandchild delivered the loaves by bike to Minnie's grown children for Shabbat dinner.
- She spent long periods grieving on a cemetery bench near her daughter Lillian's gravesite.

Getting to Know My Ancestor

The one who knows not how to question, she has no past, she has no present, she can have no future.

– E. M. Broner

Now that you know more about your ancestor it's time to dig a little deeper, searching for the meaning behind the facts. An essential part of midrash is to ask questions – who, what, when, where, how, and why – as if you were a scholar or journalist. This investigation will put leaves and blossoms on your family tree, offering an alternative to the bare-limbed, impersonal results of traditional genealogical research.

Your persistent curiosity and the quality of your questions will bring you closer to your ancestor, giving you a sense of the legacies she bequeathed to you.

Here are some of the questions that helped Gramma Minnie come alive for me:

- Why did Minnie emigrate alone as a young woman? Was she excited or terrified to leave home? Was it her choice to go? Did her family urge her to seek out opportunities unimaginable in Sanok? Did they send her away to protect her from danger?

- What skills had her mother taught her about being a woman – a wife, a mother, a human being – to prepare her for this new life?

- What motivated her return to Sanok? Were the adjustments of immigration too much for her? Was her relationship with her husband difficult? How could a young immigrant couple afford her journey, and why was it a priority for them?

- What dangers did Minnie risk traveling as a young woman without a man to assist and protect her? How did she manage alone with a baby – without a bullet train, motion-sickness medication, disposable diapers, baby aspirin, sterile changing stations, or prepared baby food?

- What did she miss most about her family? Had she ached for her father to chant a blessing and her mother to hold their first American grandchild? Was it vanity, wanting her beautiful new daughter to be admired? Did she miss the close community of her childhood? Was she unhappy in America, with her husband, with her life? Once home in Sanok again, was she ambivalent about returning to Illinois?

Homesickness became a central part of my family's culture. I never really knew who was in or out of our family – or where home really was.

– Pauline Boss

Legacy from My Single Aunts

Even in my earliest memories I embraced my individuality, that sense of being complete within myself. Perhaps this comes from being an only child. I continue to live the single life, feeling comfortable and whole. Although I once took it for granted, I now appreciate this legacy from my three aunts: permission to live a rich, single lifestyle.

Aunts Lila, Agnes, and Geneva were my dad's sisters. I knew them as single, independent, professional women. The clichés "old maid" and "maiden aunt" may occasionally have been applied by a careless cousin or thoughtless bystander, but mostly, these women were accorded a place of dignity and respect in the extended family.

Lila was my godmother, a former WWI army nurse, briefly married so long ago "it didn't count." She was eccentric and extravagant; who else would send me a cowgirl outfit special delivery on my birthday? Troubled by mood swings, she did not have Prozac to make life easier. At some point, the annual holiday visits ceased due to a family squabble. Nevertheless, she remains an example of generosity and high style in the midst of convention.

Aunt Agnes, or Addie, lived with us for the first five years of my life. While my exact memories are dim, I remember her as a free spirit. She belonged to some unnamed religious sect "where there were women preachers," long before women were allowed in the clergy. Addie liked to sleep late, stay up late, and organize things in the middle of the night. An office worker, she married another sister's husband late in life. Addie enjoyed doing what she wanted when she wanted. She was true to herself.

Geneva, called Gim, was the strongest of the three. Self-confident, she worked at everything from the Pinkerton Detective Agency to the federal government. Long before it was considered acceptable, Gim donated her body to science after her death. (Oh, such family consternation.) She was intelligent, practical, and blunt, but she did not alienate others like Lila or cause a fuss like Addie. Somewhere in old age an elderly gentleman proposed marriage, causing great merriment and prompting a quick refusal.

Did I see loneliness? No. Did I find these aunts incomplete? No. I saw three-dimensional, fulfilled human beings who enjoyed their family, nurtured friendships, and found satisfaction in their work. I am grateful to Lila, Addie, and Gim for this model of joy and dignity.

– Gretchen Heath

REFLECTION AND WRITING *(15 minutes)*

It's a good idea to do this work in a place that is special and sacred to you, using your favorite pen and lovely writing paper. You are not only honoring your ancestor, you are painting a portrait of this remarkable woman for yourself, your community, and future generations.

First, return to your notes and review your facts, assumptions, memories, and stories. Take time to read them leisurely and without judgment. Next, spend a few minutes letting the images, memories, and details float freely in your mind. Muse about your ancestor and her time in history. Consider what you know and don't know about her.

Now ask yourself: after completing my initial research, what questions do I have about my ancestor? Pondering the deeper questions will suggest possibilities that you might never have considered. Although many of your questions may be unanswerable, you will learn a great deal about your ancestor and her influence on your life.

You might use the following questions as a guide:

- Was she an immigrant? If so, why, when, and from where did she come? How was she changed by the loss of her homeland? What strengths did she bring, whether sewn in the hem of her dress or handed down through a family or cultural legacy? How did these strengths help her cope with life in a new land?

- What did she love most in her life? What was she most proud of? What were her secrets? What dream did she live or lose? What was her greatest disappointment or regret? What were her triumphs and failures? What were her strengths and limitations?

- What were her attitudes about education, beauty, faith, religion, relationships, family, responsibility, fun, illness, death? What was the most important influence on her life?

Keep searching, questioning, writing. Simply jot down each question as it comes to you, letting go of the end result. Try to write at least fifteen minutes every day. Stay loosely focused as you write, and don't concern yourself about repetition or moments when you go blank. You may wish to repeat this exercise with other family members, both male and female, weaving your ancestors into the tapestry of your life and strengthening your connection with your heritage.

Contradictory Information

The more you get to know your ancestor, the more confusing your information may seem. After viewing documents, researching facts, listening to different perspectives, and articulating your insightful questions, you probably have a collection of contradictory images. Some paradoxical information can be integrated, but other contradictions must stand side by side as different but real aspects of a unique individual. Regardless, it's important to question what you hear, even when it is said in a confident tone. If a fact, memory, or story conflicts with one of your assumptions, use your intuition to approach a more faithful version of the truth.

Grandmother, I museum you and you museum me, for what is a family but a living hall of a loved one's many faces?
– Nomi Eve

For example, my ninety-year-old uncle, the last of Gramma's children, described her as very orthodox. As much as I tried to imagine Gramma as deeply reverent and traditionally religious, nothing I knew from her life suggested that this was so. Customarily, Orthodox Jewish women either cover their hair or shave it and wear a wig. Yet Gramma spent time brushing her long, beautiful hair, and she kept a rain-collection barrel in the yard for shampooing. Intuition tells me that even though her parents observed traditional Jewish laws, Gramma did not. More likely, the words "very orthodox" reflected my uncle's discomfort with the old-world ways of his immigrant mother.

I started my search for Gramma Minnie with three words: vain, depressed, and dysfunctional. In the process of exploring the contradictions hinted at by her traveling, I expanded my picture of Gramma

My children . . .
I reach for you
across the abyss that separates our lives,
hoping you are reaching too,
knowing the differences between us,
hoping there are samenesses as well,
yearning for us to touch and know
one another.
Separated by the act of birth,
ever more distant through the act of growth,
yours, mine. . . .
May there be an ours made manifest as
our worlds move ever closer,
regaining connection,
our colors blending into a new rainbow.

– Karen Johnson Gustafson

to include very different qualities: powerful, courageous, and determined. The longer I let my curiosity play, the more connected I felt to her. Staying curious and letting myself live with the unanswerable have nourished me beyond measure. I now have a broader perspective on my life and where I came from. I have come to appreciate the ambiguities, the shades of gray in the rich tapestry of family life that I share in and will pass on to the future.

Digging beyond the facts, asking questions, and imagining her experiences, I have found a new ancestor, a multidimensional Grandma Minnie. She was not just the Torah scribe's granddaughter, the vain one with the beautiful hair. She was a woman who had the capacity to journey not once, but twice, from Sanok to create her family in America a century ago. Beyond her human frailties and limitations, I now include her strengths. I respect her story and the complexity of her life as an immigrant. I am awed by her courage and saddened by her disappointments. Cut from the same cloth, connected through time and space, I am proud to be her granddaughter.

The family that exists in people's minds is more important than the one recorded in the census taker's notebook.
—Pauline Boss

REFLECTION AND WRITING *(30 to 60 minutes)*

By now, you, too, have developed a deeper relationship with your ancestor. You've listed facts, searched for clues, and asked questions. You've compared differing perspectives and struggled with conflicting information, building a detailed composite of a remarkable woman. This exercise is an opportunity to document how your perceptions have evolved.

As you write about your unfolding relationship with your ancestor, try to work in your sacred writing space, sitting in your most comfortable chair and using your favorite pen and paper. Here are some suggestions to help you get started:

• Although my ancestor's life experience can't be confirmed with facts, I have come to these conclusions . . .

• I believe her life was . . .

- Because of what I've learned about my ancestor, my relationship with her has become . . .
- The contradictions in her life help me see that . . .
- My perception of my ancestor and her circumstances has changed in the following ways . . .
- My relationship with her has changed from . . . to . . .

Be sure to collect all the data you have gathered and written about your ancestor and put it in your binder. You will return to this information in chapter 4, where you'll decode and receive the legacies she has passed down to you.

*May you embrace
all the rich legacies
of your heritage.*

CHAPTER FOUR

$\mathcal{R}$eceiving Your Ancestor's Legacy

By getting to know your feminine ancestors you have established a vital link to the past. Before, these women may have been little more than names and dates on a family tree. Now they have come alive, revealing their strengths, hopes, sorrows, and achievements. Each of these women left a legacy to the future – to you.

Family Legacies: A Midrash

While some women are able to trace family legacies across many generations, many others are not. If access to your family history is limited, simply go back as far as you can. We all have gaps in our family history, but we can use our intuition and midrashic imagination to fill the voids.

REFLECTION AND WRITING   *(20 to 30 minutes)*

If you are working in a legacy circle, have someone read the following directions aloud, slowly and clearly. If you are working alone, you might have someone read you the directions, or you might record them yourself, pausing after each instruction.

To prepare for this visualization, choose one of your female ancestors, someone who sparks your curiosity or with whom you feel especially connected. You don't have to know a lot about her. Perhaps you've already written about her in previous exercises. Write her full name at the top of your writing paper, then set your paper and pen aside. As you listen to the suggestions, muse freely. Allow your intuition and imagination to guide you.

> *Arrange yourself so you are comfortable where you are sitting. Close your eyes and focus on your breath, following its natural rhythm . . . in and out. Notice that with each inhalation you are more in touch with yourself, you feel more centered and relaxed, and with each exhalation you let go of the distractions around you.*
>
> *Imagine that you are going back in time to the place where your ancestor lived. Give her a moment to appear. . . . Let yourself see her in your mind's eye. . . . Observe everything you can about her: her approximate age . . . her gestures and the way she carries herself . . . her facial expressions and demeanor . . . what she is wearing, how she smells. Notice her physical surroundings. Be aware of the qualities that make her who she is, both ordinary and extraordinary. . . . Take into account how she is personally affected by her circumstances . . . her culture . . . her time in history. Be conscious of her life struggles and life lessons. . . . What is she most proud of? . . . What are her greatest disappointments? . . . Who or what is she afraid of? . . . How does she express her fear? . . . Whom does she love and who loves her? . . . Think about what she is teaching her children by the choices she makes and the way she lives. . . .*
>
> *Now, for just a moment, imagine that you are stepping into her clothes and into her shoes. Take on her posture, gestures, demeanor. . . . Wear her feelings . . . incorporate her thoughts . . . embody the qualities that make her unique. . . . Experience what it is like to be her, to live her life. . . .*

She is sitting down at a simple table, gathering her pen and paper. She is going to write a letter. She picks up her pen to communicate with you directly, beyond time and space. This letter will include the things she wants you to know about her: her hopes and dreams . . . her struggles, satisfactions, achievements . . . her regrets and fears . . . her loves and joys . . . her values and ethics . . . all that matters most in her life. . . . She'll conclude with a specific message for you — an expression of her legacy, a special legacy meant only for you.

Now, open your eyes, pick up your pen, and begin to write. You may find that tears and strong emotions, hers and yours, accompany this writing. Keep writing and breathe deeply. . . . When you are finished, close your eyes and return to the visualization.

Now, become yourself again. . . . See your ancestor as she was: sitting at the table, writing to you. Take as much time as you need to thank her. . . . Say good-bye, for now. . . .

Return your awareness to the present by focusing on your breath as you did when you began this visualization. . . . Come back to yourself at your own pace. Return to this time, the twenty-first century, and to this place where you are seated writing.

Open your eyes slowly. . . . If you are alone, look around and note your surroundings, then stretch tall and breathe deeply to bring yourself fully back to the present moment. . . . If you are working in a legacy circle, make eye contact with at least one other woman.

If you are working in a legacy circle, take time to share your letter and witness letters from other women's ancestors. If you are working alone, read your letter aloud to fully take in the gift of your ancestor's legacy.

This is an especially powerful exercise, giving you a feel for the legacies left by ancestors you may have never met. Repeat this exercise as many times as you wish. You may want to reconnect with your ancestor to ask her more about her life and times, or you might explore other ancestors, female and male.

Include this letter, with an explanation, in the file for your spiritual-ethical will.

Dear Rach-e-le,

I'm delighted to write to you because I feel your love as you have come to know me. I'm proud that my love of language and reading became part of my legacy to you. I hope you will always respect both.

Another gift I bestow upon you is my love of Shabbes. I readied myself for this communal day of rest by baking challa for the families of my children. You are finding your own ways of expressing and passing down this legacy, and I am grateful that my spiritual yearning, though misunderstood by many, has blossomed in you.

Perhaps the most important legacy I pass on to you is the courage to do your life your way, to go forth *(lech l'cha)* when you need to, and to speak your mind and heart even when there's risk involved.

Be of great courage in a world that may often disappoint you. Your faith will hold you. Continue to love adventure – in travel, in books, in relationships – and to challenge tradition. You will go farther than I did. You are not disabled by the wounds of immigration; your generation enjoys many opportunities that mine did not. Make the most of them.

Know that I love you and I am with you, and will be for the rest of your life, my granddaughter, Rach-e-le.

– Gramma Minnie

Difficult Legacies

Of the many legacies we've received, some feel like gifts, others like karmic burdens. Though our ancestors didn't wish to hinder us with difficult legacies, the fact is that conflict, trauma, secrets, and human frailties exist in every family. Unfortunately, injuries that occur often affect subsequent generations.

By writing about difficult legacies, we often come to understand the influence they have had on our lives. For example, a woman who realizes that a distant relative gave birth out of wedlock may finally realize the source of the silence and shame handed down through her family line. The survivor of domestic violence may discover that her grandmother also suffered maltreatment at the hands of a husband or parent – a cycle of abuse to be repeated for generations. Understanding these legacies can release us from painful or destructive patterns that have been unconsciously handed down for decades, even centuries. It allows us to transform them not only for ourselves, but for those who come after us.

I was fifteen when I took up my grandmother's legacy. That year, the story she had planted in me – a haunting, tremolo note – which I carried throughout my childhood as a pit in my belly, ripened, in the same way that my hair turned from yellow to brown.

– Carol Edgarian

REFLECTION AND WRITING *(30 to 60 minutes)*

Choose one of your feminine ancestors. She may be someone you've already written about or someone new. Begin by writing her full name at the top of your paper. Now, reflect and write notes on the possibility that she has bequeathed you:

- An unresolved issue from her life
- A lesson or value from her unique life experience
- A trait or preference that both of you have struggled with

When you are finished, look through your notes and choose one legacy to explore. As you reach back through time, you will begin to grasp how some essence of this legacy – a value, lesson, character trait, or unresolved issue – has

Dear Mary Eileen,

Today I want to share my sadness with you as well as my hopes for you. So much that I wanted in my life – as a young woman I was full of enthusiasm and excitement – never came to fruition. I felt alone and different, neither understood nor respected. Part of that was the increasing distance between me and my children. They were intent on fitting in, becoming Americans, and they poked fun at much that I cared about. And my husband, your great-grandfather, was a powerful man plagued with anger and alcohol, like his father before him. Nevertheless, he became a model for the boys, and the girls adored him.

I felt old before my time, like I was the receptacle holding all the grief and loss for everyone in the family. Life was hard. I worked long hours caring for nine children who rarely cared about me. They left prairie life for the city as soon as they could. I didn't have the strength to weather it all. At some point I just gave up and became resigned to loneliness and the death of my dreams.

But you must not give up. Let your dreams transform you – don't let the inevitable losses of life destroy you. May you have new and powerful dreams, and may your dreams come true.

– Your great-grandmother, Mary Margaret

been handed down through your family. Concentrate your writing on recovering, reconciling, reshaping, and redeeming this essence.

- What facts or family stories contribute to your understanding of this legacy?
- What questions are evoked by these facts and stories? Are there gaps or inconsistencies in this information?
- How has your life been affected by this legacy? How does this legacy clarify your understanding of your own behavioral patterns?
- Would you choose to pass this legacy on to your family and community? Why or why not?

Revisiting Sarah

Up until now you have immersed yourself in your personal past. You have touched your feminine ancestors and received their legacies – some welcome, some difficult – handed down through generations of women. Before moving your attention to your present life in part 2, let us return for a moment to our ancient matriarch, Sarah from Genesis. Because Sarah is an archetype, she will mean something different to each of us.

We know the truth of Sarah's life story not because it appears in sacred Scripture, not because we can prove that it happened in a particular time or place or even that it happened at all, but because Sarah's story somehow belongs to us. Every woman can see elements of her life in Sarah. Her story is our own story, issuing from deep within us.

We yearn to reclaim the feminine legacies of our multigenerational past, whether we are dispossessed or securely linked to our ancestors. As we explore our unique connections to Sarah, we realize that we are part of the collective human tapestry. Through Sarah, even women who are separated from their family histories can reconnect with their roots.

Each of us is the distillation point of a great funnel in time that consists of the history, culture, and evolution of our species.
– Denise Linn

One's self is rooted, among other things, in one's history and one's heritage.
– Pierre Sauvage

REFLECTION AND WRITING   *(20 to 30 minutes)*

Like all of us, Sarah made mistakes and poor choices. Her life was filled with joys, regrets, triumphs, disappointments, and hard-learned lessons. In this exercise, you will explore your feelings about Sarah and the legacies she left to you. Before you begin, you may want to review Sarah's story and reread the letter you wrote for her in chapter 2.

Now, imagine that Sarah is your great-great-great-grandmother. Recount the legacies she bequeathed to you, jotting down notes as you reflect. Record your thoughts and feelings about these legacies. Consider how Sarah's legacies affect you today, how you feel about them, and any revelations you have had about Sarah, yourself, or legacies in general.

~

When I want to read a culture, I listen to stories about families, sensing in their contours the substance of larger mysteries.

– Toni Morrison

Before we move on to part 2, it's time to take stock. You now possess all the writing tools you will need to create your spiritual-ethical will: letter writing, question-and-answer lists, midrashic imagination, and freestyle writing. You will call upon these methods as you work through the rest of this book.

Take time to record your thoughts about connecting with Sarah, your ancestors, and your family history. Gather these gifts from the past so you can consciously apply them to the next leg of your journey: an exploration of who you are today.

We've explored the importance of our names. We've confronted our yearning to be connected, to feel that we belong. We've witnessed and honored the legacies left by our feminine ancestors – gifts of history, gender, and genetics. Now we turn to our own lives.

In the chapters that follow you will reflect on your personal journey, seeking connection to all women while honoring that which is unique and extraordinary within you. You'll paint a portrait of who you are: your childhood and adolescence, feelings about your body, work and play, friendships and secrets. You will celebrate your gifts, grieve your losses, and examine your identity in relation to long-held notions of women as both mothers and sexual beings. Finally, you'll consider your spiritual nature and how it sustains you in a patriarchal culture.

Having a sense of self or identity is a necessary prerequisite to creating a legacy. Before you can give your stories, values, and wisdom to the future, you must gather yourself, articulate who you are, and celebrate the sacredness of your life.

May this be a journey of discovery, acceptance, integration, and celebration.
May you be transformed and renewed as you prepare
to create your spiritual-ethical will.

PART TWO

The Present ~

May you find guidance
in your quest for
self-knowledge.

CHAPTER FIVE

$\mathcal{W}$ho Are You, Really?

Gathering of self requires a quiet, courageous heart that is willing to explore long-ignored aspects of your identity. The exercises in this chapter are meant to support your discovery. Each is designed to tap something valuable inside you – memories, feelings, sights, sounds, smells – to help you know yourself more fully. Your goal is to assemble your self and add it to the "you" gathered from your family history. After you complete each exercise, take notes about any insights you gained from your reflection and writing. File your writings with your other spiritual-ethical will materials.

Home

We begin with a sense of place, of home. In Jungian psychology, the house symbolizes the personality. Dreams that take place in the basement of a house may yield information about the individual's foundation, or basic character, while the attic symbolizes her mind or spirit.

The house, the garden, the country you have lost remain forever as you remember them.
– *Eva Hoffman*

We reveal a great deal of ourselves in the way we make a home and endow it with our energy. Through our homes we express our values – simplicity, beauty, creativity, safety – and each home radiates an energy that affects all who live there.

Though we didn't create our childhood homes, they nevertheless influenced who we are today. Some of us will recall our homes as warm and nurturing havens of safety; others will remember home as scary, unpredictable, even dangerous. To understand who we were as children, we must explore long-buried memories related to our homes. Consider your childhood home as a kind of safe-deposit box, for which this exercise is the key.

REFLECTION AND WRITING

This exercise is used with the permission of Sally and Huey Crisp, writing instructors from the University of Arkansas at Little Rock. In addition to your usual writing materials, you will need an unlined, blank piece of paper and a pencil with an eraser.

~ *Part 1*   *(10 to 20 minutes)*

Begin by thinking about the home you lived in when you were growing up. If you lived in more than one, choose the one that first comes to mind or the one where you spent a significant amount of time from ages three to twelve. Take a moment to let the home appear in your mind's eye. See its exterior, its doors and windows; notice the area surrounding your home.

Now, use your pencil to draw a floor plan of this home, numbering each room. Include significant outdoor elements such as steps, trees, gardens, fences, a garage, a shed, or a yard. You can erase and make changes as necessary.

As you draw, memories may begin to flow. Jot down a word or phrase to remind you of each memory. You may write inside the rooms or on a second sheet of paper, noting the room numbers so you can connect rooms with memories later on.

When you're finished making notes, take a few moments to write about each memory. Be as specific as you can, capturing smells, tastes, sounds, and sights. Sensations will revitalize your memories. Even the most mundane memories — what you ate for breakfast on school days, the household chores you enjoyed or despised — will help you recover who you were as a child.

"I recall the safety and comfort of the little paneled den with the TV, where I often took meals on a tray and relaxed and recharged before homework," writes Susan Eastman Tilsch. "I recall the living room with the bay window and the oval rug, where Robert Frost one afternoon came for tea. The sun porch where my father, in anger, pushed me into the glass window. My brother's bedroom where I watched a terrible struggle of physical will between my father and my brother. My mother's bathroom where all of us children were freely invited to talk to her while she soaked in the tub. The front hall where I threw up after holding in the nausea of a day at school. My other brother's bedroom where I remember him propped up on his bed studying his physics textbook with total joy and intrigue. My older sister's bedroom where I remember feeling proud of my input as I helped her brainstorm for a high school English paper. As I thought of the kitchen, I found no warm memories there. My mother had never enjoyed cooking. And the dining room was where my father fell asleep at the table. My mother said he was tired and later we learned he was drunk. I recalled my own bedroom with its pink and white wallpaper and its own bath and the wonderful dollhouse that my father built out of bookshelves, which, with their open structure, allowed me to reach my dolls from all directions."

Childhood memories illustrate your unique history while informing your future. Like Susan, you will have a wide range of memories — some painful, some precious. If you want to examine a specific memory, try the freestyle writing technique from chapter 4. You might also experiment with repetition, contrast, alliteration, or other writing techniques. Use your senses to recollect a particular time or place: the sound of music coming from the kitchen, the smell of lilacs in the spring or holiday cookies baking in the oven, the mustiness of the storage room, the monsters hiding behind the furnace in the dark basement, the sounds of anger or laughter that you heard while in bed.

Feel free to examine other memories from your childhood. You might, for example, draw floor plans of your elementary school; the local library; a hospital where you or a family member were treated; the buildings where your parents worked; or the church, synagogue, or mosque of your youth.

To conclude this exercise, write some notes about who you were as a child and how your childhood experiences influenced who you've become. When you're finished, file your writing in a safe place. At the end of section 2, you will review your writings to create a portrait of the unique and complex woman that you are.

Role Models

But I was sixteen years old and worried enough about keeping my own physical balance. One false step and I might fall off the edge of the world. I was afraid to walk the outer limits.

— Faye Moskowitz

If you are like most women, role models have played an important part in your life, particularly in your youth. Friends, mentors, teachers, and famous people in film, music, and politics all may have left their imprint on your personality as you journeyed through adolescence.

This three-part exercise, beginning with a simple list of names, is an opportunity to recall yourself after childhood and before adulthood, a time of excitement, exposure to new ideas, and discovery of who you were in relation to the world beyond your home and family.

REFLECTION AND WRITING

~ *Part 1*   *(5 to 10 minutes)*

Make a list of people who were important to you as a teen. Consider your heroines and heroes as well as people whom you considered wise. Your list may contain teachers, coaches, clergy, friends, relatives, famous people, and characters from your favorite books and films. Include role models who had either a positive or negative effect on your life.

~ *Part 2* *(10 to 20 minutes)*

Choose one of the role models from your list, then write about any of the following:

- What attracted you to this person? How did gender play a role? How did age play a role? What was your relationship like?
- What values did you admire in this person? Were these values similar to or different from your parents' values?
- How did this person influence who you are today – your relationships, career choices, attitudes and values, political beliefs, and community or global concerns? Before moving on to part 3, you may want to repeat this step and write about other people on your list.

~ *Part 3* *(no time limit)*

Check your list to see if there's anyone from your adolescence with whom you've lost contact but would like to reconnect, whether in person or in writing. You may want to tell this person about his or her influence on your life. Consider writing a letter to articulate what the relationship meant to you. Let yourself express your appreciation or disappointment. If you choose not to send the letter, file it with your other writings.

When you've finished with this exercise, take a few minutes to record your thoughts and feelings. Use this time to step back from your adolescent self and evaluate what you have learned. Through your writing, you may have come to see yourself and your role models differently.

My Body

On the wall of a massage studio at Clare's Well, a spiritual retreat center, is this anonymous statement:

After a certain number of years, our face becomes our biography.

– Cynthia Ozick

In the glory of the morning remember your womanbody.
And remember that whether your body is abundant or slight,
Somewhere in the world a goddess is venerated
Who looks exactly like you.

For some of us, the idea that our bodies are sacred is difficult to accept. Poor body image begins early and seems unavoidable in our culture. It is a vicious cycle that affects how we feel about who we are.

As adolescents, we prayed to the "mirror, mirror on the wall," hoping to hear magical confirmation that we were the fairest of them all. It didn't happen. Instead, the mirror pointed out to some of us that we had straight hair when everyone we admired had curls; we had tiny breasts, and the boys all noticed those with curvaceous, womanly bodies; or we were curvaceous and wanted our bodies lithe and boyish. We were too short, too tall, too fat, too thin.

Many decades later our bodies continue to be sources of dissatisfaction, carrying the blame for any number of failed relationships and opportunities. Could this explain the millions of dollars spent each year on tummy tucks, face-lifts, breast implants, and countless other cosmetic surgeries? Are we seeking something more than youth and beauty, perhaps agelessness and immortality? If we succumb to the technology because it exists and we can afford it, have we abandoned some deeper part of ourselves? Why is it so difficult to celebrate our unique physical bodies?

As an aging woman, I am momentarily thrilled when someone says, "Oh, you don't look sixty." Then I feel guilty, because the part of me that is pleased with the compliment is simultaneously sabotaging myself and other aging women. And what will it mean when no one says that anymore? If I "look my age," is that not beautiful?

Just when we get used to our bodies the way they are, they change. And with each change, we must update our images of ourselves.

We reclaimed our bodies,
inch by precious inch.
Feeling our own skin,
astonished, like touching
a newborn.
– Ellen Bass

I don't like to think of
them as chin hairs. I think
of them as stray eyebrows.
– Janette Barber

Consider how your body changed from that of a young girl to a woman with breasts, hips, a waist, and body hair. Perhaps you also experienced a pregnant body, followed by menopause and an aging body.

Though some of us may prefer otherwise, living requires a body. Bodies house our pain; express our competitive, sensual, and erotic natures; and carry our souls through the world. Some women use their bodies as instruments of coordination and strength, expressing themselves through exercise, conditioning, and athletic mastery. Other women, seeking different avenues of expression, see their bodies as burdens or impediments. Still others use their bodies in ways that degrade them, employing their physicality to gain power. Some even use their bodies to inflict self-punishment – overeating, starving themselves, cutting themselves, or denying themselves physical touch and affection.

As long as our bodies continue to serve us and don't demand our awareness, we tend to take them for granted. But when our bodies are in dis-ease, we are required to pay attention. Illness may be the first time we take responsibility for our bodies and their care. And this, paradoxically, may be the start of our appreciation for our bodies' beauty and complexity.

Take care of your body. This is very important.... And treat your body with the reverence and care God did in blessing you with it.
– Sharon Strassfeld

REFLECTION AND WRITING   *(45 to 60 minutes)*

Take time to reflect on your relationship with your body. Then, after reading the questions below, let yourself muse, your thoughts unfold. Write freely to clarify who you are as an embodied person.

- Consider the history of your body. Have you been healthy or ill? Have you ever felt betrayed by your body? Have you ever abandoned your body?
- Do you pay attention to the basic needs of your body, inside and out? Consider food, sleep, exercise, walking, bathing, breathing. What are your expectations for your body?

- What part did body image play in your early feminine development? How does the cultural norm of "thin is beautiful" help or hurt the way you treat your body? What biases do you have about bodies, yours and other women's?

- In what ways do you enjoy your body? Does your body bring you a sense of joy and competence, allowing you to participate in sports, dance, yoga? What is your favorite body part? How has your body been a source of fear or shame? How do your attitudes manifest in your body? How have you used or abused your body? How have you paid a physical or emotional price for this use or abuse?

- What skills and gifts have you derived from your body? What has your body taught you about yourself? How has your body contributed, positively or negatively, to your sense of self-worth? Has your body distracted you from finding and knowing who you really are?

- How has your relationship with your body changed over the years?

- What does your body mean to you today? What feelings do you have about your body as you age?

- How do you understand yourself as a body/mind or a body/mind/spirit? How do you demonstrate your respect and appreciation for your body? Do you consider your body a sacred vessel that houses your spirit, literally carrying you on your life's journey? Why or why not?

When you've finished this exercise, take a few minutes to document your writing process. Include insights that help you define who you are, and note areas where your attitudes about your body are in transition. File your writings in a safe place for later review.

An Old Story

Getting older? Me too. I'm not old. Forty-six isn't old. Just older. It's right about in the middle. It's older than young but younger than old. That's what forty-six is. My body gives me clues – slight alterations slipped into the daily fabric of my life – to let me know I'm moving along, chronologically speaking.

Like my skin. It's getting too big for me. Lord knows I've had my problems with my skin. But not fitting has never been one of them. My skin has always fit me. Even when I was hard to fit. Even when I shot up really fast. Somehow my skin knew to expand proportionally with my growth spurts. Somehow my skin knew to do its thing.

Now, if we were talking about clothes, we'd have that oversized suit taken in. Why, we wouldn't be caught dead in our one-size-too-large suit. Like my one-size-too-large birthday suit. And if that weren't bad enough, the fact of the matter is that my birthday suit fits the best it's ever going to fit. If I keep going at this rate, it won't be long before I'll have enough skin to outfit Shaquille O'Neal.

Yes, I'm a woman on the move. There's no stopping my rather rapid descent into the pavement. Because that's where all my skin is headed. Downward. Gravity's way of putting meaning into my epidermic life. Then my discs begin doing their thing, and the rest of my body catches up – I mean, down – with my skin. I'm like the genie going back into the lamp. Shrinking . . . ever . . . smaller.

Maybe that's why old people walk so slowly. Because their bodies are wrapped around their ankles. And I see this tendency in myself. Even at forty-six. It's looking more and more like I'll outlive my skin. And then where will I be? Ten centimeters from my bunion?

Yes, my body gives me clues at forty-six. Little clues, slight alterations slipped into the daily fabric of my life. . . .

– Gale Kaplan

My Work

Living on this earth demands that we *do* as well as *be,* and for most of us, our doing is at least partially defined by our work. In this patriarchal society, where the value of *being* is absent, our worth is generally measured by success and achievement in the workplace. More important, however, is our own personal satisfaction in any work done to the best of our abilities.

It's inspiring to witness women in legacy circles talk about their work. Hostility toward housewives and full-time mothers melts away. The defensiveness of stay-at-home moms evaporates. Frustrations begin to ebb as young women who are trying to do it all listen to the wisdom of experienced elders. Judgments about whose work is more important disappear as women reveal their deepest commitments to life. Some women share their struggles to balance working outside the home with managing a household, raising children, and partnering. Others discuss their volunteer work, their peace work, their desire to make the world a better place.

No matter what kind of work we do, each of us makes an important contribution to *tikkun olam,* repairing the world. An important tenet of Judaism, *tikkun olam* obligates us to continually do what we can to make the world a more just and caring place, knowing it is impossible to complete the task in our lifetime. All women, regardless of their faith, can fulfill this commitment to *tikkun olam,* whether at home, in the workplace, through volunteerism, or through art.

Volunteerism, though often devalued, is a necessity in our society. Many women spend years working as volunteers, teaching children to read, serving meals to the homeless, caring for the sick and the aged, helping at food shelves and shelters, and maintaining all manner of nonprofit, charitable, and religious institutions.

The pitcher cries for water to carry and a person for work that is real.
– Marge Piercy

It is not your obligation to complete the task of perfecting the world, but neither are you free to desist from it.
– Pirke Avot 2:16

Creating beauty is yet another way that women heal the world, though many artists, poets, and craftswomen are not valued for their work. Like volunteers, they rarely have jobs that pay good salaries, and they are seldom embraced by the industrial or corporate world. Nevertheless, their work is often significant and thought-provoking, bringing beauty to their communities and inspiring momentous changes within individuals as well as society.

Raising children, of course, is a unique opportunity to contribute to a better world. Though the task may seem all-consuming at times, parenting allows us to teach compassion, service, generosity, and other ethical and spiritual values. And the jobs we work to pay the bills are an equally important contribution. Even when a woman's job has no deep meaning for her, she is still making a difference – perhaps putting food on the table for her family or paying the medical bills for an aging parent.

And what does retirement mean for women? Does it mean that once a woman is sixty, or sixty-five, or seventy, she doesn't work anymore? No. The thought of time stretching out before us, free of the requests and needs of others, may be terrifying, thrilling, or both. Yet for many of us, retirement suggests that we finally have a chance to do our real work, the work we were meant to do. Remember, Grandma Moses painted for the first time as an older woman. Harriet Doerr's first novel, *Stones for Ibarra,* was published when she was seventy-three.

When Toni McNaron, first chairperson of the groundbreaking Women's Studies Department at the University of Minnesota, retired after thirty-seven years of university teaching, she saw not an end, but a beginning. "Although I am about to sever all official ties with the university that has been my professional home for so long, I know in my heart that I am not fleeing where I have been – but racing toward whatever destination might be next."

My second favorite household chore is ironing. My first being hitting my head on the top bunk bed until I faint.
– Erma Bombeck

It's important that you love your work. Never stay with a job just because it's a job. Work at things that you love and that fill up your life.
– Sharon Strassfeld

Yesterday I hung my wash out to dry. It was a heavenly act, one I had first experienced when living in Cambridge, Massachusetts. With the smell of fresh, sun-dried clothes I was transported back to 1962. I remembered the game I'd devised, pinning up each item in a precisely chosen order so the sun would find it attractive.

Rather than use the dryer at the laundromat, I would lug my wicker basket, heavy with wet sheets, towels, and underwear, up to the back landing of our third-floor apartment. There I'd attach each item to the line with weathered gray clothespins, then use the pulley to move the wash across the yard away from the house. In winter the laundry would flap and slap, often frozen to stiff attention by the nor'east wind. Even in the cold I had felt unhurried, delicious, like I was part of eternity. In the summer I'd stand peacefully in the sun, holding clothespins in my mouth, deciding where to pin each item so as not to leave a mark on a shirt.

This experience was lost long ago, forgotten in the rush of modern life as I balanced home and work, all the while praising God for the luxury of a clothes dryer just a step away so I could fix dinner, schedule a client, make a grocery list, and juggle so many other things. Now I wanted to string a clothesline in my backyard so my sheets could go straight from the sunshine onto my bed. But the passion was in the memories. . . .

I recalled living in Tunisia, where the laundry lines were draped with hand-woven and hand-dyed cloths – opulent orange, brilliant purple, and rich red – drying in Saharan siroccos. I would hang my son's diapers on the flat rooftop of our third-floor walkup, just outside the walls of the medina. Hand-wrung after being washed in the bathtub, they bleached whiter-than-white in the North African sun.

I recalled my childhood and the awe we felt when our first automatic washer arrived on Newton Avenue. The old wringer-washer sat ignored and shamed in the corner as we oohed and aahed, watching the soapy bubbles in the window of the magic Bendix. At nine years old I had no idea how this new laborsaving device would change women's lives.

And in my mind's eye I saw women bent over rivers in all places and all times, washing clothes, spreading them on rocks to dry in the sun, and I knew myself a part of the timeless community of women. I wondered, did Rachel wash clothes at the well where she watered flocks and first met Jacob so long ago?

REFLECTION AND WRITING   *(45 to 60 minutes)*

Let yourself write freely about any of the questions that follow. Remember, these questions are meant to stimulate, not constrict, your thinking.

- What is the history of your work life? What was your first job? How did you feel about it? What did you learn from it?

- What do the words *job, career, profession,* and *retirement* mean to you? What are your attitudes and expectations about work? If you have children, which attitudes do you want to teach them? Why?

- What is your attitude toward domestic work? How has your attitude changed over time? How has domestic work defined you?

- What skills and gifts has work given you? What price have you paid for your achievements?

- How has work distracted you from finding and knowing who you really are? Has work been a source of difficulty as you balanced your other needs and responsibilities?

- If you have spent time in the workplace, what have you learned about yourself? Have you tried to fit yourself into a structure antithetical to your nature – struggling for equality or dealing with sexual harassment, lack of respect, or the glass ceiling? If so, how has this affected who you are?

- If you come from the generation of stay-at-home moms and housewives, how do you define your work, and what does this work mean to you? How have you fared as a woman of the "bridging generation," subjected to centuries of patriarchy and the natural inclination to care for the home, yet torn by the desire or need to work outside the home? How have you integrated these contradictory influences? What biases do you hold about the "right way" for women to work in the world?

- For some women, "doing" and "achieving" make them feel worthy. If this is true for you, describe your experience – your work, time spent working, your workplace, and how work has influenced who you are. What is your vision of positive and authentic work in your future? How has work been a source of your development, your ability to express yourself and your values? If you are committed to repairing the world, how has work been an opportunity to fulfill your obligation?

Playfulness

Having discovered the significance of work and how it defines us, we turn now to its counterpart, play. We might define play as leisure activities – social events, concerts, hobbies, movies, travel. But playfulness is also a state of mind, a sense of lightheartedness and humor that defines our perspective.

Whether you consider yourself playful or serious (or both), having fun is a universal longing. For some women, reflecting on play brings a sense of nostalgia, a yearning for the freedoms of childhood. For others, childhood was a time of hard work and obligation; only now, as adults, can they consider learning how to play.

You know the hardest thing about having cerebral palsy and being a woman? It's plucking your eyebrows. That's how I originally got my ears pierced.
– Geri Jewell

REFLECTION AND WRITING *(45 to 60 minutes)*
Reflect on yourself as a person who enjoys life, someone who experiences humor and fun. Then, let yourself write freely about any of the following questions:

- How has play defined or eluded you throughout your life? What are your attitudes and expectations about play, humor, and having fun today? Consider hobbies, crafts, games, sports, reading, films, concerts, and social time with friends. How has your relationship with play changed over time? How do you visualize authentic play in your future?
- What did you play with as a child? What skills and gifts has play given you? How has play been a source of your development? In which aspects of your life do you use humor to express yourself?

- What does fun mean for a woman of your generation? What priority does play have in your life, given your values and obligations? Must you work before you feel entitled to play? Has personal enjoyment been a source of guilt in your life? If so, how has this affected who you are?
- What has been the cost of play in your life? Has play distracted you from finding and knowing who you really are? What biases do you hold about the "right way" to play or the appropriate place for humor in the world?
- How have you made time for fun at different stages in your life? What feelings do you have about humor and play as you age?

Travel

They were also carriers of an internal legacy that originated long ago in another part of the world. This was a tradition whose visible signs Jews reestablished wherever they went.

– Eva Hoffman

I am a proud American citizen, and, like the purple-and-green trailing plant, I'm also a wandering Jew. Most of my life I have experienced myself as "other," always different, wandering in the desert, seeking the Promised Land. My sojourn as a Peace Corps volunteer in Tunisia was a daily adventure, sometimes fun, often difficult, and always a learning experience. Later, during my visit to Israel, I had the thrill of walking as one of the majority through streets that boasted King David manhole covers and Twelve Tribe taxis. Both Tunisia and Israel changed my perception of who I was and am.

Many women travel not just for fun and relaxation, but as a way of linking the present to the past; they might trace their family histories and stand in the very places where their feminine ancestors once lived. Others travel to learn about the world, to experience global citizenship, to appreciate the beauty and rich variety of cultures, art, food, and nature. If you define yourself, in part, by such travel experiences, this exercise will be an opportunity to explore a unique aspect of yourself.

For other women, travel has been painful or difficult. They steer clear of it whenever possible, opting instead for the safety of home and belonging. Many of these women moved frequently as children due to a parent's job relocations, military transfers, or employment struggles. Some women have avoided travel because of financial or health reasons. Others have traveled as refugees, escaping religious or political persecution. Of these women, many arrived on rickety boats or in the holds of ships, not on the decks of cruise liners. They came with little money and few possessions. Learning a new language and culture was about survival and hardship. If you are one of these women, this exercise will be an opportunity to explore the wounds of travel and document the inner resources you developed to persevere.

There are stories we tell ourselves over and over, all of our lives. These stories, verbal vertebra, spine our minds — helping us stand, if not straight, then at least only a little bit crooked.
— Nomi Eve

REFLECTION AND WRITING   *(60 minutes)*

For this exercise, you may want to gather photographs, ethnic music, or other travel mementos to inspire you. Begin with a simple list of the places you've visited or sojourned, whether countries far away or the town next door. Choose one of these places to write about.

- What did it feel like to be among those whose language, daily life, perspective, and culture were different from your own? Write about feeling "other."
- What did you like or dislike about this place? What did you find deliciously different and comfortably common? Include special memories you connect with this place.
- What personal strengths and limitations did you discover while traveling (curiosity, courage, and confusion, for example)?
- How do you anticipate and prepare for travel?
- How do you feel when you travel? What does travel mean to you?
- Consider the meanings of home and immigration. How have these defined who you are?

Knowing Myself

We don't see things as they are, we see things as we are.
– Anaïs Nin

Theresa of Ávila said, "The path of self-knowledge must never be abandoned." In a sense, self-knowledge is a primary goal of this book. You've already gained vital insights to help articulate who you are – a preliminary step to creating your spiritual-ethical will. This exercise poses specific questions about your most hidden self.

REFLECTION AND WRITING   *(10 to 15 minutes)*

The following list will help you examine some of the situations and relationships that define who you are and what matters most to you. Choose one phrase that sparks your interest. Write that phrase at the top of a fresh sheet of paper and complete the thought in your own words. Let your mind explore the truth of your statement, writing about any thoughts or feelings that arise before your allotted time is up.

- What I have loved most about my life is . . .
- My greatest disappointment in my life is . . .
- What I regret most about my life is . . .
- The greatest lesson I have learned is . . .
- A time in my life when I was courageous was . . .
- The deepest question I have about my life is . . .
- A film, musical composition, or piece of art that has had great significance in my life is . . .
- A fairy tale, children's story, fictional character, or book that has had an important influence on my life is . . .
- An elementary or high school event that had an important influence on my life was . . .

When you are finished, take a few minutes to decide what to do next. You may want to continue writing on this topic, write about another phrase, or move on to the next exercise.

Endings

One thing we don't do well in our culture is clarify or honor endings. It's true that some endings, like childhood, can't be marked by a specific moment in time. These are hard to recognize and ritualize. Other endings are only recognizable by a new beginning: the first day of school, first kiss, first airplane flight, first time driving a car, first time falling in love, first paycheck. And some matters, like being a daughter, never really end, though certainly there are endings and new beginnings within this aspect of one's identity.

Most of us would rather focus on the future to avoid the pain and loss associated with endings. But if we don't examine our endings, we lose the opportunity to understand how they affect who we are. Without our attention, endings are just happenings, incidents that we push away as if they have no meaning.

Consider the implications of endings in the natural world: a tree dropping its leaves in autumn, the snake shedding her skin, a caterpillar enclosing herself in a cocoon. How have endings transformed your identity?

> *A new year can only begin because the old year ends.*
> *– Madeleine L'Engle*

> *Re-vision – the act of looking back, of seeing with fresh eyes, of entering an old text from a new critical direction – is for women more than a chapter in cultural history: it is an act of survival.*
> *– Adrienne Rich*

REFLECTION AND WRITING *(45 minutes)*

Write about something that has ended in your life. Choose something simple; you can tackle the more complex endings after you practice with easier ones. Consider:

- The end of a specific day, holiday, vacation, or season
- The end of a job or career
- The end of an era: elementary school, high school, adolescence; turning thirty, fifty, sixty-five
- Leaving your home, city, country, or homeland
- Divorce, death, or the end of a relationship

Describe how the ending occurred and how you responded. What did you think and feel? Did you allow yourself to grieve? Do you still have unfinished business related to this ending? What do you regret? What do you appreciate? Did you create a "completion ritual"? Write about possible ways to honor and finalize this ending. What did you learn from the ending? How has it defined you?

Change

Inside every older person is a younger person — wondering what the hell happened.
— Cora Harvey Armstrong

Some life changes are dramatic and complete, while others are experienced as an evolutionary process. Menarche, for example, is a distinct biological moment, but the transformation from girlhood to womanhood takes many years.

Change – transformation – is at the heart of our identities. By tracking our transformations, we clarify who we are and what we value, discovering lessons that we might not learn in other ways. In some cases, transformation is a kind of deliverance. Many women, for example, are enslaved by addiction, illness, abuse, a job, an unhealthy relationship, or a negative self-image. Such slavery has long-term ramifications, degrading us and binding us in victim roles. When deliverance comes in the form of recovery, remission, or release, it can be a powerful, redefining experience.

It's difficult to understand the significance of deliverance when we're in the midst of it. With the advantage of 20/20 hindsight, we can better appreciate our deliverances and the lessons learned along the way.

REFLECTION AND WRITING *(45 to 60 minutes)*
Begin by making a list of changes you've experienced throughout your life. Consider the biological and psychological, the slow changes and the dramatic changes. Any defining event can be transformative, including the loss of virginity,

menopause, a medical diagnosis, or a spiritual awakening. Choose one such transformation, then write about the following:

- Describe your transformation. How did it happen? Who were you
  before, during, and after it occurred? What did you learn during each
  part of the process?
- Do you consider this transformation a kind of rebirth or deliverance? If
  so, how do you understand the purpose of this deliverance?
- How has this transformation affected your sense of who you are? Does
  it continue to influence your identity?

You may want to write about other transformations on your list as well.
Take a few minutes to reflect on how transformations have influenced who you
are today.

World Events as Defining Moments

I was a young schoolteacher on November 22, 1963, when President
Kennedy was killed. Subsequent to my personal loss and mourning, I
vowed to serve in the U.S. Peace Corps, taking seriously Kennedy's
words: "Ask not what your country can do for you, but what you can
do for your country." This experience transformed me, and it continues to affect my life today. I became a world citizen in those two
years, learning a lot about the universal hopes and dreams of women
as I, an American Jewish woman, lived, worked, and socialized in
Tunisia, a North African Muslim country.

All sorrows can be borne if
you put them into a story
or tell a story about them.
– Isak Dinesen

We don't often look at history in terms of personal identity, but
in those rare moments when the entire world stops – in surprise, in
shock, or in horror – we are all transformed. And we are all connected. At these times, each of us belongs to something larger: our
culture, our world, our times.

Knowing who you are provides insulation against the onslaughts of a random universe.

– Barbara Kessel

"The way we deal with each of these moments," writes Joan D. Chittister, of the Order of Saint Benedict, "determines who and what we really are, who and what we are intended to be, who and what we can become both spiritually and socially. . . . Like everyone ever born who goes through sudden, defining loss of any kind . . . women find themselves faced with the question: Who am I when I am no longer who and what I was?"

REFLECTION AND WRITING   *(30 to 60 minutes)*

List world events – war, terrorist attacks, the AIDS epidemic, or the assassination of a prominent leader, for example – that have influenced who you are today. Explore one of the events on your list. Consider the following questions:

- Where were you when you first learned of the event? What did you do, think, feel? Were you alone? How did you find solace and hope?

- Did you participate in community activities, memorials, or prayer services in the days that followed? Did you volunteer your time, your money, your blood?

- Who were you before and after the event? How did your life change? Has your life been in a state of flux since the event?

- What regrets do you have about the event or your responses to it? Have any blessings come out of the event?

- Do you have unfinished business related to the event? If you've not had closure, is there something you can do to memorialize the event so you can move on? Consider creating a ritual to promote remembrance and reverence.

You may wish to write about other world events that have affected you. Before you set this writing aside, consider what you want to communicate to your loved ones about the meaning of these events and how they changed you.

Friendship

Our friendships sustain and define us. They balance our needs for privacy and solitude with our need to connect with others. Even when friends disappoint us, we value them as much as family and lovers.

In *Journal of a Solitude,* May Sarton examines the nature of her relationship with a dying friend. "Deep down," she writes, "there was understanding, not of the facts of our lives so much as of our essential natures." Friendship is built on this understanding, an unspoken contract maintained through time, distance, and all manner of personal change.

Separate reeds are weak and easily broken; but bound together they are strong and hard to tear apart.

– The Midrash

REFLECTION AND WRITING *(20 to 45 minutes)*

Write about any of the following. You may want to continue this writing over several days, examining one topic in greater detail or exploring the different components of friendship.

- Reflect on the value of your friendships throughout childhood, adolescence, and adult life. How has the nature of your friendships changed over time?
- How do you maintain friendships, particularly with those who live far away?
- Consider these challenges: letting go of a friend, building a relationship with a new friend, changing your relationship with an old friend.
- Do you have a best friend? What is the essence of that relationship?
- What do you value most about your friendships? Are there values or actions that you won't tolerate in your friends? In yourself?
- How have you betrayed friends? How have friends disappointed you?
- What changes would you like to make in your friendships?
- Describe your essential nature – your values and special qualities. How do you feel when you are "met" in your essential nature, and when you meet a friend in hers?

Families

Family knowledge can be useful in making abstract history concrete.

– Eva Hoffman

Many women have two families, the one they grew up with and the one they created with a partner. Although these families may be very different from one another, both have a profound influence on our lives. Families shape vital aspects of our identities – who we are as daughters, granddaughters, sisters, nieces, aunts, mothers, and grandmothers – and we, in turn, shape our families.

REFLECTION AND WRITING *(20 to 45 minutes)*

Compare and contrast your growing-up family and the family you co-created, or write about your own definition of family. You may continue this writing for several days before moving on to the next exercise. Consider the following suggestions, or simply follow your intuition to explore different aspects of family.

- What special memories do you have of a grandparent or grandchild? How are these relationships unique?
- Which family members have had a strong influence in your life?
- What is the defining story of your family?
- How have family holiday rituals or spiritual activities changed over the years? Which traditions have you maintained?
- How does your family cope with illness? How have responses changed over time?
- How does your family express a sense of humor?
- Is your family close? How have family members maintained their connection?

My Mother's Song

We tied the line
    between strong trees
        clear across our yard
I gave her pins
    one by one
        as she gave me her song

Clothes caught the song
    billowed
        and snapped against the sky
Leaves rustled the song
    and birds
        tossed it like a bouquet

Now I sing a song
    a tall tree song
        a soft blue memory
wrapped in the clothes
    she washed and smoothed
        and draped in the sky for me

              – Patti Tana

Secrets

Whether painful or glorious, secrets are part of who we are. Secrets held too long, however, can be a destructive force in our lives, all the more dangerous because we don't often see their influence. Writing about secrets may bring release and healing, but it also creates the risk of exposure. If you choose to write this exercise, you might decide to keep your writing private, neither sharing it in your legacy circle nor including it in your spiritual-ethical will.

Many secrets are borne of shame, a sense that we are bad, ugly, cold, selfish, cruel, unloving. We believe we have a history or quality that makes us "other" and thus unfit for the human community. Alcoholism, extramarital affairs, abortions, and children born out of wedlock are often "shameful" skeletons kept deep in the closet – so deep that many women aren't even aware of their long-lasting effects.

Fear is another factor. Some women are afraid they will endanger themselves or others (often their children) if they expose their secrets. This is particularly prevalent among women who have been abused: they often believe, perhaps accurately, that silence will protect them.

In *Sacred Legacies,* Denise Linn writes candidly about the effects of secrets on our lives: "Secrets can take on a life of their own. They can create 'territories of the unspoken,' where there are tacit rules that those subjects can never be discussed. Often there will be some family members who know the secret and some who do not. This division creates covert alliances to keep the secret. Those who don't consciously know of the secret are still deeply affected by its negative influence on their psyches. . . . Children know and feel the unspoken; they have an inner radar for the forbidden, dark secrets of a family. . . . Writing about the mistakes in your life and the family secrets, which everyone knows and no one speaks about, can be healing for you and can offer understanding for those who follow you."

REFLECTION AND WRITING

While doing this exercise, many women discover that they've been abused verbally, emotionally, physically, or sexually — secrets they've kept even from themselves. If you decide to go ahead with this writing, you may find that you need help processing the information. If necessary, seek professional help from a qualified therapist or spiritual advisor.

The act of writing can liberate you from the burden of your secrets. Moving a secret from your heart to paper can even help resolve old fear or shame. Some secrets you carry may not even be yours, though they have undoubtedly affected your life: perhaps a feminine ancestor shared her secret in a letter, or you might have understood it intuitively through the visualization in chapter 4.

You may have legitimate fears about writing down your secrets. Much of this fear may be left over from a time when you were young and vulnerable. Remember, you have more power now than you did then. You alone will determine how to write your secrets (in code, private shorthand, or traditional narrative form) and what you will do with the writing when you are finished (save it, share it, shred it, or burn it). Make sure you have a safe and private place to store your writing until you complete this exercise.

You may choose to skip this exercise. If you wish to continue, take time now to reflect on your purpose for doing so. Remember, your ultimate goal is to discover who you are and what you value so you can effectively communicate your personal legacy.

Because of the high emotional voltage inherent in this exercise, do not write for longer than the suggested time limit.

∼ *Part 1*   *(10 minutes)*

Make a list of secrets, yours and your family's, that may have affected your life or the lives of others. When your time limit is up, stop and reflect for no more than ten minutes. Record your thoughts and feelings, including shame, fear, relief, and release. Wait a day before beginning part 2.

~ Part 2   *(20 minutes)*

Choose one secret from your list in part 1 and review the following questions. These questions are meant to guide your exploration of a highly charged subject.

- In *Thunder and Lightning,* Natalie Goldberg suggests writing "to record how you saw and felt before you were silenced." What was your life like before you had this secret?

- When did the secret begin? How long have you known about it?

- How has this secret affected your life, both positively and negatively? (Sometimes what feels like a curse turns out to be a blessing.) How has it affected the lives of others?

- Do you think there is a way to resolve the secret today? In the future?

- What are the advantages in confiding your secret to others? What are the potential risks in exposing the secret to family and friends? What will become of the secret once you have told it?

- What is the difference between keeping a secret and guarding your privacy? Compare the isolation, hopelessness, and loneliness brought by secrets to the quiet, restorative, inspirational benefits of privacy.

Repeat this exercise as needed, allowing no more than one writing session per day. Pay close attention to the time limit. After each session, take ten minutes to consider how this writing is affecting you and determine how best to take care of yourself. Be sure to keep your writings in a secure place.

~

You need only claim the events of your life to make yourself yours.

– Florida Scott-Maxwell

Each exercise in this chapter has helped clarify a different component of your identity. You might reread your writings and make some brief notes to get an overview of the influences that made you who you are today. When you have finished, set these writings aside. At the end of this book, you'll incorporate your writings into a unique spiritual-ethical will.

~

*May you be blessed
with gratitude for being
born a woman.*

~

CHAPTER SIX

Woman, Mother, Sexual Being

Viewed through the lens of patriarchy, female biology gives rise to two social roles for women: mother and sexual object. While mothering and sexuality are basic to feminine nature and essential for the survival of humanity, womanhood is far too rich and complex to be reduced to these elements. Nevertheless, history has regarded women as child bearers, caretakers, and objects of sexual possession. Birth, nurturance, and female sexuality have been much maligned, and the "feminine" has been distorted to serve the "masculine." Women suffer collectively and individually because of the misogyny endemic in societies governed by dominance rather than partnership. For too long, there has been silence or ridicule about the value – and values – of women.

While Western society has become somewhat more enlightened in recent decades, we cannot ignore the damage done by centuries of male domination. Most women today struggle with a sense of diminishment related to sex and mothering. Some women have inherited a legacy of limited self-worth, a belief that they exist only to take care of others – their children, their partners, their aging parents. Other

*Many of us are living out the
unlived lives of our mothers,
because they were not able to
become the unique people they
were born to be.*

– Gloria Steinem

women have gone to the opposite extreme, shunning motherhood
and intimacy altogether.

Love, nurturance, protection, passion, and sensuality are precious
traits essential to our humanity. Before we can leave our legacy to the
future, we must value that which has been devalued: we must learn
to love and honor ourselves as mothers and sexual beings.

All Women Are Mothers

In *A Woman's Worth,* Marianne Williamson writes, "We don't have to give
birth to children to know we're the mothers of the world. We are the
wombs of the generations that follow, not only physically but emotionally, psychologically, and spiritually. . . . We are all mothers to all children."

As twenty-first century women living in the West, we have had
more choices, more control over our bodies than women at any other
time in history or around the globe. Though you've likely made different choices than your mother or your grandmother, you may discover that your feelings and values about mothering connect rather
than divide you.

*My mother wants me to know
what happened, and I keep
every detail of what she tells in
my memory like black beads.*

– Eva Hoffman

We have all given birth – to a child, an idea, a work of art, ourselves.
We have all nurtured and protected our creations and the people we
love. To understand what mothering means in our lives today, we need
to explore the powerful and often contradictory feelings we have about
motherhood.

The following exercises will help you discover what being a mother
means to you and how it has affected your life. You will explore where
and how you fit into the community of mothers, how social expectations
have affected you, and how mothering is a unique component of who
you are, whether or not you have birthed or raised children.

REFLECTION AND WRITING

~ *Part 1*   *(10 to 20 minutes)*

According to *The American Heritage Dictionary,* to mother means to "give birth to; create and produce" or "watch over, nourish, and protect maternally." With this definition in mind, write down everyone and everything you have nurtured and protected (a child, your partner, parents, pets, plants, yourself) as well as the things you've created and watched over (art, crafts, ideas, projects, programs, companies, gardens).

~ *Part 2*   *(15 to 60 minutes)*

Read through the following prompts to explore the abstract and practical components of motherhood. Then, write about those aspects that interest you the most.

- Is mothering a woman's job? How is it different from fathering? From parenting?
- What does "mother love" mean to you? Where and how did you learn about mother love? When and in what circumstances have you received mother love? How do you express this love?
- How have expectations – yours and others – affected your sense of yourself as a mother? Do you mother willingly, or out of a sense of obligation or necessity? Do you feel adequate to the task of mothering? Have you valued or devalued yourself for your mothering?
- What have been the rewards and sacrifices of mothering? How has it been a gift in your life? How has it been a duty, an obligation? What have you learned about yourself through mothering?
- What is the purpose of mothering? What is the power of mothering? How is mothering a unique expression of who you are?
- Consider your mothering experiences in the light of historical, ethnic, traditional, and family influences.

When a subject evokes strong emotions, give yourself permission to experience the depth of your feelings. One way to acknowledge feelings when writing is to fold a piece of paper in half. Write your reflections on the right side. Name your feelings on the left. Legacy circle participants have found it possible to write and weep simultaneously, and they have read their deepest-felt writings through choked-up throats and tear-filled eyes.

Mothering Children – Or Not

Listening to our mothers' stories is the beginning of understanding our own.

– Naomi Ruth Lowinsky

The traditional definition of motherhood, of course, relates to the birthing or raising of children. Whether or not you have traveled this road, your life has likely been touched by any number of social or biological concerns: abstinence, birth control, infertility, pregnancy, miscarriage, abortion, labor and delivery, adoption. Here you will explore how these issues have affected your perception of motherhood.

REFLECTION AND WRITING   *(30 to 60 minutes)*

Muse on the following topics, then examine the questions that most interest you. Write for no more than an hour a day, and take as many days as you need.

- Have you experienced any of the following: birth control, hysterectomy, miscarriage, infertility, pregnancy, delivery, termination of a pregnancy, fertility medicine, adopting a child, placing a child for adoption, or being the mother of a blended or foster family? How have these been sources of grief and joy, difficulty and fulfillment?
- If you do not have children, whether by choice or circumstance, how has this affected your sense of yourself as a woman? How have you felt pressured or supported by family, friends, society?
- Have you yearned for a child and felt desperately hopeless that it would never happen? If your life has been touched by infertility, how has it affected you? How have you come to terms with your own expectations? The expectations of others?

A Balancing Act

Reconciling the experience of mothering with other aspects of life is a daunting, often confusing task for many women. No matter what your age, education, family customs, social position, or economic circumstances, trying to balance motherhood with your personal dreams may pull you apart. Here you will explore how motherhood fits with the rest of your life – and how external pressures complicate the tension that exists between caring for others and caring for yourself.

The community of women that once supported a domestic life of mothering is no more. At one time, women spent their days with other women, washing clothes at the riverbank while children played nearby and infants slept contentedly in the sun. Today we "throw in a load" before driving to work or carpooling kids to after-school activities. We try to do it all, bouncing back and forth between exhaustion and frenzy.

Amid the many demands of motherhood, it's easy to lose sight of our personal aspirations, even as we derive a special satisfaction in nurturing others. In *Fear of Fifty,* Erica Jong describes her own surrender to motherhood – its gifts and frustrations – and the interruption of her creative life:

"Years after giving birth, I became a mother against my will because I saw that my daughter needed me to become one. What I really would have preferred was to remain a writer who dabbled in motherhood....

"It humbled my ego and stretched my soul. It awakened me to eternity. It made me know my own humanity, my own mortality, my own limits. It gave me whatever crumbs of wisdom I possess today....

"Those women who have given up work, art, literature, the life of the mind, for nurturance naturally resent those women who have not had to. The privilege to create is so new for women. And the privilege to create and also nurture is newer still. Those women who have given up nurturance feel resentful too."

I have yet to hear a man ask for advice on how to combine marriage and a career.
– Gloria Steinem

The phrase "working mother" is redundant.
– Jane Sellman

You decide to have a baby and end up with a range of feelings that run from the rapturous to the murderous (with four thousand stops in between).
– Ellen Goodman

Marking Him

Does my little son miss the smell
of his first mother? I wonder,
as the mew of his mouth
opens toward a plastic bottle
which is not her breast.

In her good-bye letter to him
sealed in his album
with a birth certificate which now
lists my name as Mother,

his first mother writes
she nursed him briefly
after he emerged into
the second room of his world.

    I think of milk volcanic
and insistent, answering
the newborn's gigantic hunger,
a primal agreement between
generosity and greed.

Sometimes
I press my nose
to the glass of that place
where a mother and my child
belong to each other;
I cannot imagine coming
between them.

Sudden new mother,
I bury my nose deep into
his skull cap of ringlets,
his starry cheesiness,
want to lick him all over
with a cow's terry-cloth tongue,
to taste him and mark him as mine

so if the other mother returns,
she will repeat the doe rabbit's
refusal of the kit I handled.
Whiffing the baby,
smeared with my smell,
she won't take back my child.

– Margaret Hasse

REFLECTION AND WRITING   *(30 to 60 minutes)*

Use the following questions to stimulate your thinking about the contradictions between your mothering and other aspects of your life. Continue writing on this topic for as many days as you choose, but write for no more than an hour a day. Sharing this writing in your legacy circle may call up new topics to explore.

- For centuries, women's short lives were filled with childbearing, nursing, cooking, cleaning, weaving, sewing, and fieldwork. Have you experienced the never-ending work of mothering and domestic life? If so, how have these been a source of rebellion, satisfaction, creativity, boredom, or resentment? How does mothering fit into your daily life, whether or not you have children?

- Many women pursue higher education, a career, a calling – paths that women in other times and places might not have even dreamed of. What opportunities have you had that your mother and grandmother did not? What difficulties have you encountered in balancing motherhood with other paths you have chosen?

- How have economics defined and affected your mothering? Have single parenting and underemployment limited the time you can devote to mothering? If so, how?

- How has privilege or deprivation – due to government policies, racial bias, or patriarchy – determined your views of motherhood and your ability to mother? Have you hired others to care for your children so you can work outside the home? How do you feel about this? If you are a nanny or daycare provider, what are your feelings about mothering other people's children?

- What paradoxes do you see in your life as you balance mothering with your other dreams? What gifts and frustrations have you encountered? What have you sacrificed in your commitment to mothering? How have you sacrificed mothering in favor of other aspects of your life?

- How does mothering affect your evaluation of your worth as a woman and a contributing member of the human community?

A Theology of Motherhood

A theology of motherhood —
a theology it is.
Rich with myth, illusion, reality,
woven together, indistinguishable,
one from another.
We speak with cautious certainty
even as we speak of God —
as though someone, somehow, somewhere
knows the truth.
We grasp for answers
that elude us like milkweed seeds
floating freely through the air,
alighting at random,
sending up new shoots,
and on and on.
And how much closer are we really?
Babies and mothers
born together,
each unique yet evermore the same.
What do we know?
What can we trust?
What is the truth that sets us free
to be what we can be?
Unbound, unbonded we are alone;
bound and bonded we are confined.
Where is the middle ground
that finds us whole
and one
with one another
and our God?

— Karen Johnson Gustafson

Mothering and Menopause

Today, few women believe that we exist merely to birth and raise children. Nevertheless, menopause often makes us question our value, even when we've chosen not to have children. What is our worth when our childbearing years are over?

Feminist and feminine spiritual writers contend that with menopause, our greatest worth is just beginning. In *New Passages,* Gail Sheehy suggests that as males' hormone levels deplete in midlife, women's testosterone levels are rising. This accounts, in part, for the creativity and vitality that women experience in their sixties and seventies. No longer considered old, many women experience a second energetic adulthood at this age. Legacy writers describe this time as vital, hopeful, active, creative, and spiritual. Perhaps freed by an emptied nest and the pressure to compete as sexual objects, we are pregnant with ourselves, creating our own lives, maybe for the first time. With the wisdom of experience and the freedom to be creative, older women are committed to self-development and to making a difference in the world.

I am no longer anybody's child. I have become the Grandmother.... The rhythm of the fugue alters; the themes cross and recross. The melody seems unfamiliar to me, but I will learn it.

– Madeleine L'Engle

REFLECTION AND WRITING   *(30 to 60 minutes)*

As you read through the following, consider your expectations, ideas, and feelings about menopause. Write for no more than an hour, and take as many days as you need to complete this exercise.

- How do you view menopause – as a beginning, an end, or both? Describe your fears and expectations, whether or not they've been realized.

- If you have reached menopause, what do you see before you? How has your creativity expanded at this stage in your life? How does menopause change your role as a mother?

- If you have not reached menopause, how do you feel about the future stretching out before you? What new opportunities or limitations do you envision at this stage of life?
- How do you view your worth as a woman and a member of the human community when your childbearing years are over?

The Contradictions of Motherhood

How do you feel about mothering? This exercise offers an opportunity to explore your joys and sorrows – all your conflicting emotions – related to motherhood. Consider who or what you have mothered, what kind of mother you are, and what you love and hate about mothering.

Nobody can make you feel inferior without your permission.

– Eleanor Roosevelt

REFLECTION AND WRITING   *(45 to 60 minutes)*

Use the letter-writing technique to communicate your thoughts and feelings on this complex subject. Writing a letter keeps the paralysis of perfectionism at a manageable level. You've already used this technique in chapter 2 when you wrote a letter for Sarah, and again in chapter 4 when your ancestor shared her legacy with you.

You may choose not to share this letter with anyone. Although your ultimate purpose is to communicate your legacy, this writing is meant to deepen your understanding of who you are. Later in the book you will decide whether to share this letter as part of your spiritual-ethical will. In the meantime, keep it with your earlier writings.

Decide to whom you might write this letter. Begin with a personal greeting and this opening phrase: "My dear _____, I want to tell you what it has been like for me to be a mother. . . ."

Sexuality: A Curse or a Blessing?

Physical love, no matter the sex of our partners, becomes sacred when it is an expression of the deep longing we have to experience the Divine in one another.

– Joan Borysenko

Used to celebrate life and love, women's sexuality cannot be bad, ugly, or sinful, yet it has been abused and distorted throughout history. In our earliest cultural myths, women fulfilled their "destiny" to have children, to populate the world, to assure the continuation of humanity. The Scriptures are full of stories of sexuality and power, barrenness and inheritance, exploitation and betrayal. Even in the Garden of Eden, we are told, God punished all women with pain during childbirth because Eve seduced Adam with the forbidden apple. (Where was Adam's responsibility?) And our old friend and first matriarch, Sarah, was used as a sexual possession and gift when Abraham feared for his life.

The damage done through centuries of patriarchy is not easily overcome. Technology has given us complex responsibilities and new choices, yet women continue to fight for sexual freedom and equality. We battle for recognition of our sexual choices – whether to have children, same-sex partners, the single life, the celibate life. We struggle for equality in our intimate relationships, where many women are not yet full partners. We seek protection from abuse, we press for changes in the way society views aging women. In some parts of the world, women still struggle for inheritance rights, the right to initiate divorce, the right to be seen unaccompanied in public.

And the day came when the risk to remain tight in a bud was more painful than the risk it took to blossom.

– Anaïs Nin

Women's sexuality has indeed been a curse at certain times in history and in certain parts of the world. But it has also been a blessing, because our sexual nature is at the root of our creativity and our spirituality. Our attitudes about sexuality, of course, come from our family and friends; our culture, society, and religious community; and our own life experience. Some of these attitudes are healthy and liberating, while others are harmful and oppressive. In this exercise you will explore the source of your own attitudes toward women's sexuality.

Using the following questions as a starting point, write about your feelings, thoughts, and memories. You may wish to continue this writing over several days, keeping to the time limit. When you have finished, record your reactions to the writing process.

- Reflect on your sexual history. Who were you as a girl? What messages about sexuality did you receive from the men in your family and community? From the women? From your feminine ancestors?

- Consider your education about sexual biology. What messages did you receive about your body? What did you learn about your sexual body parts? What was the prevailing attitude about bodily care and respect in your home?

- What, when, and from whom did you learn about appropriate sexual behavior? How were rules about dress and bodily care related to sexuality? What sexual rules and roles did you learn from your family? From classmates and friends? From your ethnic or religious community? What sexual behaviors were permitted or prohibited, whether alone or with others of either gender?

- Were you a "good" girl or a "rebellious" girl? Were you chaste, promiscuous, disinterested, or frightened of sexual activity? Write about the sexual experiences you had as a child, an adolescent, and a young woman.

Sexuality and Relationships

When I was a teenager, friends would call to cancel plans because a boy had asked them for a date. Each time, I felt angry and hurt. I wondered why boys were more important than girls, and I swore I would never abandon my friends like that. But once I fell in love, I did. Nothing came before that relationship; it was the only thing that mattered.

I think — therefore
I'm single.
– Lizz Winstead

No Kissing

Once they start kissing,
people stop talking.

"No kissing for three months."
She rubbed the length of him.

"We can hug, of course,"
she purred into his ear

"You didn't just kiss me, did you?"

Her head dipped as she demurred,
hair touching his arm,
tickling out a tiny gasp.

He lifted her head,
fingers tracing her face,
resting for a moment on her upper lip
and then gently tripping lip to chin.

And still they didn't kiss.

Instead he parted his lips and drew in a breath
as if to sigh some sweet regret.
She opened her mouth to protest
and his sigh slipped between her lips
and entered her.

— Beverly A. Lutz

I regret it to this day, because it was my friendship with myself that I ultimately betrayed.

Sexuality has a way of sneaking into our everyday relationships. Like it or not, friends, family, coworkers, and even strangers may be affected by our most private affairs, though often in quiet ways. Consider how this dynamic operates in your life.

It is easier to live through someone else than to become complete yourself.
– Betty Friedan

REFLECTION AND WRITING   *(15 to 30 minutes)*

Examine any of the following topics. This writing may evoke strong feelings, so be sure to seek needed support from a confidante, professional counselor, spiritual advisor, or the women in your legacy circle. To explore your thoughts and feelings on this complex subject, you might fold a piece of paper in half, writing your thoughts on one side, feelings on the other.

You may complete this writing over the course of several days. Be sure to honor the daily time limit. When you are finished, record your thoughts, feelings, and insights about what you wrote, then file your writing in a safe and private place.

- How has sexuality affected your relationships with friends, family, yourself? When and how have you sacrificed one relationship for another?
- How have you used your sexuality to get what you wanted or needed? How have you used or abused your sexuality at work, in relationships, or with your family?
- What messages from family, sexual partners, society, or religion have influenced your friendships and intimate relationships? Write about positive and negative messages you have learned, whether real or imagined.
- How do you feel about Freudian theories that suggest men's sexuality is more acceptable than women's sexuality? How have these theories affected your beliefs about gender and relationships?

- Write about sexual abuses you observed or experienced as a child, an adolescent, a young woman. Have you discussed these abuses with others – perhaps a friend, partner, family member, therapist, or clergy person? How have these experiences influenced your relationships, sexual identity, behaviors, and attitudes? How have they affected your integrity as a sexual person?
- Are you troubled by your sexual feelings or inhibitions? How have sexual misunderstandings altered or limited relationships in your life?
- What beliefs about your own sexuality have limited your capacity to participate in a loving sexual relationship? Have you experienced your sexuality as fully as you would like in your intimate relationships?
- Write about your most special intimate moments. Did you feel that you were fully yourself? That you and your partner were one? That you were expressing your love of God or life?

Honoring Sexuality and Gender

People call me a feminist whenever I express sentiments that differentiate me from a doormat or a prostitute.
– Rebecca West

As you explore your feelings about sexuality, you may be overcome by a sense of gratitude for the freedoms that women have today. Or you may grieve, knowing that sexuality is still used to oppress women, often violently, around the world. Wounded or not, sexuality is fundamental to women's creative and spiritual energy. It is the foundation of our strength, our art, our ability to form loving relationships with ourselves and others. This exercise is an opportunity to discover a new level of understanding and comfort, perhaps reclaiming sexual power that has been lost or distorted.

REFLECTION AND WRITING *(30 to 60 minutes)*

Explore any of the following to discover or reclaim your sexual nature:

- Which of these common sexual descriptions do you believe are generally true of women, and which do you attribute to yourself: manipulative, teasing, innocent, dangerous, shy, inhibited, uninhibited, liberated, frigid, dominant, submissive, insecure, self-assured, seductive, faithful, unfaithful, responsible, irresponsible, sensual, sinful, withholding, healthy, promiscuous, appropriate, oversexed, undersexed? Are you surprised by the descriptions you've chosen? Where did you learn to feel this way? Are you satisfied with your perceptions, or would you like to change them?

- Have you ever felt wounded or powerless because of your sexuality? If so, what have you done to heal yourself, to regain control?

- What is the purpose and value of sensuality in your life? What has been important to you about your sexuality?

- How respectful are you of your sexuality, sensuality, sexual behavior, and sexual relationships? Have you valued or devalued the power of your sexuality?

- The Latin root of intimacy, *intimus,* means "innermost." Do you believe there is a spiritual aspect to intimacy? How has your sensuality or sexuality linked you to something larger than yourself?

- In what ways has sexuality been a gift in your life? What have you learned from it? Consider how your sexuality is a unique expression of who you are.

- What can you do to celebrate your sexuality, alone or with others?

The Essence of Woman

Womanhood, of course, goes beyond mothering and sexuality. Each individual has qualities that make her unique and qualities she shares

If high heels were so wonderful, men would still be wearing them.

– Sue Grafton

I thought blonde women knew

I dyed my hair
because
I believed it was the key the ticket the price of admission
to the room with doors closed and curtains drawn
to the circle
where the Secret was spoken aloud
and passed like Communion wafers on a plate
from one woman to the next.

I dyed my hair
and walked down the aisle on the arm of a man I barely knew
waiting
for the person with the Answer to stand up please
because now I'm a woman a wife a lover
and I'll make needless mistakes
unless someone will tell me.
Can't you see I'm floundering flailing
failing.

I dyed my hair
and waited for children
and answers
believing that surely
at the next stoplight
on the next bus
at the next scheduled meeting
of the next death-defying group
a letter would arrive
with my name
written in a familiar hand.

My mother never told me . . .   – Nancy Lundborg

with women around the globe. We can't help but ponder the essence of femininity, appreciating our power, delighting in our strengths, and acknowledging our weaknesses as we map the core of our characters.

To many women, "femininity" is a distasteful term loaded with oppressive connotations. But what is the true meaning of "feminine"? The answer to this question takes us beyond the socially imposed notions of womanhood to an authentic examination of our gender, our humanity, and our individuality.

Whoever thought up the word "Mammogram"? Every time I hear it, I think I'm supposed to put my breast in an envelope and send it to someone.

— Jan King

REFLECTION AND WRITING

~ *Part 1*   *(5 to 10 minutes)*

Make a list of words that suggests the essence of womanliness, qualities you regard as "feminine." Include every adjective, noun, or phrase that comes to mind, even those that contradict one another. Record clichés and unusual qualities, those that you prize and those that bring shame.

When you are finished, read your list aloud. If you are working with other women, go around and around the circle, each woman taking a turn to name one quality from her list. If you hear a quality you hadn't thought of but want to include, by all means add it. You will find a partial list, compiled by legacy circle participants, on page 114.

~ *Part 2*   *(20 to 30 minutes)*

Record your thoughts and feelings about the list you've created, then consider these questions:

- Which qualities on your list have traditionally been used to describe women? Which accurately describe you? Do you have qualities that you consider unique?

- You may decide that you've named human qualities that men have as much potential to develop as women. How does this clarify or confuse your understanding of the feminine?

Accepting	Doubting	Lost	Sensitive
Aloof	Earthy	Lover of beauty	Sensual
Angry	Emotional	Loving	Sexual
Artistic	Empathic	Loyal	Silent
Authentic	Exclusive	Moody	Smart
Beautiful	Fierce	Multitasker	Spiritual
Bitter	Flexible	Naughty	Storyteller
Brave	Forgiving	Needy	Strong
Cheerful	Friendly	Open	Studious
Clever	Frightened	Overbearing	Submissive
Communicative	Frigid	Passionate	Subtle
Compassionate	Fun–loving	Perceptive	Superficial
Complex	Generous	Persistent	Survivor
Compliant	Gentle	Playful	Talkative
Confined	Genuine	Poetic	Tenacious
Contemplative	Gossipy	Powerful	Tender
Contemptuous	Grief-stricken	Practical	Tired
Content	Grounded	Realistic	Tolerant
Controlling	Helpful	Receptive	Tough
Courageous	Honest	Reflective	Trusting
Creative	Hopeful	Refreshing	Underdeveloped
Curious	Humorous	Resentful	Unforgiving
Demanding	Imaginative	Resilient	Unseen
Depressed	Inclusive	Resourceful	Visionary
Determined	Intuitive	Responsible	Weary
Direct	Jealous	Responsive	Wicked
Disappointed	Judgmental	Rigid	Wise
Discouraged	Kind	Ritualistic	Wistful
Diverse	Listener	Self-reliant	Worn
Dominant	Lonely	Sensible	Worrier

- How have your feelings about the feminine been affected by prevailing views within our culture? Which qualities do you appreciate, clandestinely or openly, in yourself or others?
- Are women more likely to be seen as feminine if they are heterosexual? If they're part of a couple? How do such cultural biases affect a woman's sense of wholeness? How might these biases relate to the problems faced by older women, who are often considered invisible or worthless? How can single, lesbian, widowed, and divorced women express their feminine nature?
- Note how you feel about your list and about women in general. Are your reactions celebratory and proud, or sad and disappointed? Which qualities do you admire? Which are you ashamed of? How has your perspective about women changed as you've considered these qualities?

~ *Part 3*   *(20 to 45 minutes)*

Reflect and write about your own feminine qualities, particularly those that define who you are beyond clichés and traditional gender roles. Give yourself the freedom to appreciate your complexity, the natural coexistence of your opposing qualities. Consider the qualities you celebrate and those you feel ashamed of.

~

May the Divine grant
you and your writing
authenticity and meaning.

~

CHAPTER SEVEN

A Woman's Spiritual Journey

Spirituality is that dimension beyond the biological, beyond the tangible, that gives our lives purpose. Some people define spirituality as the inner self; others see it as a relationship with a higher power that calls us to be fully who we are. For many people, our deepest needs define our spirituality: the urge to seek meaning, the yearning to make a difference with our lives, the longing to give back to the earth and the communities that have blessed us.

This chapter focuses on discovering and clarifying who we are as spiritual beings. We are ready to take this step, having done the self-discovery work in chapters 1 through 6. As Joan Borysenko writes in *Pocketful of Miracles,* "We cannot give up our sense of self-importance and move beyond the limits of 'I' and 'mine' until we have a sense of self to begin with. A common pitfall in the search for identity and union with the Divine is taking a 'spiritual bypass.' In our hurry to give up the ego, we fail to go back and analyze our [life stories], heal our wounds and reap the wisdom of our pasts. Until this is done, we have not moved fully into our egos, so we cannot consciously move out of them."

Around the world, women embrace Western and Eastern faith traditions, New Age spirituality, esoteric wisdom, ancient goddess practices, Twelve Step programs, and many other belief systems. For others, nature is the fount of spiritual connection. Some women describe themselves as agnostic or atheist. Still others continue to search but have yet to find a faith tradition that fits.

Each of us has her own beliefs and allegiances. As we examine the people and events that have influenced our spiritual development, we enrich our understanding of our most deeply held values. We learn to appreciate who we are and how we came to be.

In the pages that follow, we'll trace our spiritual histories and map our sacred journeys. We'll explore prayer and ritual, betrayal and forgiveness, purpose and meaning. But first let us examine our childhoods, which were often times of powerful spiritual connection before reason and other cognitive skills kicked in.

Childhood Beliefs

I remember thinking that if God had anything to say to me, he would write me a note on lined paper – the grainy kind we used for penmanship practice in second grade during World War II – and put it under my pillow. I was always disappointed when I looked for the note in the morning. It made me worry that I was not very important to God, because if I had been, he surely would have contacted me.

This memory clarifies who I thought God was when I was a child. He was a he. He was smart. He had a long white beard and wore long robes. He sat on a throne similar to the maroon, velvet-upholstered chairs in the second-floor lobby of Radio City Theater, long torn down, in Minneapolis where I grew up. And, most significantly, he was not interested in communicating with me.

Everything has its wonders,
even darkness and silence, and
I learn, whatever state I may
be in, therein to be content.
– Helen Keller

The road to enlightenment is
long and difficult, and you
should try not to forget snacks
and magazines.
– Anne Lamott

REFLECTION AND WRITING   *(45 to 60 minutes)*

To stimulate your earliest recollections of the sacred, choose from among the following. When you are finished writing, remember to take notes on your thoughts and feelings about what you wrote. Repeat this exercise as many times as you wish.

- Recall your childhood room, its contents, how you felt there. What were your spiritual experiences, your thoughts about God, when you lived in that room? Go into other rooms in your childhood home seeking spiritual memories. Record dreams, nightmares, and other experiences about the mysteries of the universe or your beliefs about God.

- Describe your earliest spiritual experience, your first direct encounter with the numinous. Where was it? How old were you? Were you alone? Did you tell anyone about it? Has this kind of experience happened to you since childhood? If so, describe how the experiences were similar or different in their power or meaning.

- Remember your favorite childhood stories, fairy tales, or books. Do you see a theme — a belief or value — that runs through these stories? How does the theme relate to your spiritual life today?

- What were your beliefs about creation, heaven, hell, or spiritual purpose? What did your parents believe, and how did they directly or indirectly communicate this to you? How did their beliefs influence your spiritual development? How have your beliefs changed since?

- How old were you when you experienced your first death? Was it someone in your family? Was it a natural death of old age, a death from severe or life-threatening illness, or the tragic death of someone "too young to die"? How did your family communicate with you about the death? What grief rituals did your family practice? How were you included or excluded? What did you understand then about death — why that death, why any death? What did you learn about the value of life and death? The meaning and purpose of life? An ordered or random universe?

- Was there anyone you talked to about unanswerable questions? What was the foundation of your spiritual beliefs? What did you learn about who you were, the world you lived in, religion, God's power, God's goodness, unanswerable mysteries?
- How was the inexplicable handled by your older siblings, your parents, your grandparents? What did you learn from teachers, spiritual leaders?

Losing or Leaving Your Faith

The highest goal of spiritual living is not to amass a wealth of information, but to face sacred moments.

– Abraham Joshua Heschel

Many women have left the religion of their childhood. Some express anger at the patriarchal system that diminished their worth or deprived them of full participation. Others were disappointed that the creeds seemed more important than one's relationship with God or the needs of people in times of crisis. Though many women feel it was right to leave, some now sense a spiritual hole in their life. They yearn for the support of and connection to a spiritual community.

REFLECTION AND WRITING

~ *Part 1*   *(30 to 60 minutes)*

If you have left your faith, consider why and whether the decision is still what you want and need. Have you adopted a more satisfactory set of beliefs and rituals? Write about how your current belief system meets or fails to meet your needs.

~ *Part 2*   *(60 minutes)*

Reflect on relationships you have lost due to death, divorce, moving, or job changes. Consider your major disappointments and failed dreams. Examine the most difficult times in your life – serious illness (yours or a loved one's), unexpected moves, job losses, accidents, attacks, and traumas. Then, write about any of the following. Afterward, record your insights and feelings related to this writing.

- How and what have you grieved? How has your belief system supported you in difficult situations? Have you healed, or is your grief unfinished? How have you integrated your losses?
- Have you adapted to a new reality, found a "new normal"? How have your losses and disappointments changed your values and principles, your ideas and ideals related to yourself, others, life, death, God?
- Have you coped with your losses alone or in a community? What kind of assistance have you needed or received from others?
- How are your losses and your resulting beliefs a part of who you are today? Reflect and write about the effects of loss on your spiritual life and development.

You may have a number of losses and disappointments that you want to consider in depth. Repeat this exercise as many times as necessary.

A Spiritual Journey

I can recall several incidents from adolescence that stunted and delayed my spiritual development. For example, I was lied to, told that "we don't light Sabbath candles because when we go out the house might burn down." On Yom Kippur (Day of Atonement), when I asked questions about God's existence, I was called an atheist. I was punished: sent to my room and barred from attending the most important holiday service of the year. How did these events affect my spiritual life as a young woman? I cut off my questions and renounced interest in anything remotely related to religion. I'd abandoned my spirituality so completely that when I decided, at age fifty-five, to experiment with lighting Sabbath candles, it felt more than rebellious. It felt revolutionary – and terrifying.

Today I believe that God is simultaneously the still, small voice within me and the impersonal, unknowable source of creation. Both

It's so much easier to write a resumé than to craft a spirit. But a resumé is cold comfort on a winter night, or when you're sad, or broke, or lonely, or when you've gotten back the test results and they're not so good.
– Anna Quindlen

*Observing the Sabbath is
like having a steady date
with God.*
– Marianne Williamson

*Our spiritual and religious
lives depend on the stories
we choose to tell and how
we tell them.*
– Rabbi Sandy Eisenberg Sasso

beliefs, though contradictory, are part of my personal theology. But when I am really scared for myself or others, I pray passionately for God to fix what I can't. Afterward I feel foolish, realizing that the God I prayed to was the God I had hoped for as a second grader, the one who could intervene if he chose to.

Spiritual development happens over many, many years and encompasses all the values we've held in a lifetime. In crises, it's natural to revert to earlier behaviors and beliefs. We can better understand the complexity of our spirituality by exploring how our images of God and answers to spiritual mysteries have evolved as we've matured. Knowing our spiritual histories also helps explain why we carry contradictory, even paradoxical, images of the Divine. Moreover, it helps us understand why we revert to earlier developmental patterns when we are in crisis.

In this exercise you will draw a road map of your life to highlight events, people, and experiences that have influenced your spiritual development. This map plots your unique journey. It will help you see where you are, where you've been, and maybe even where you're going.

REFLECTION AND WRITING

You will need a large sheet of unlined paper and some colored pens for this exercise. Draw a line down the center of the paper. Use horizontal hatch marks to divide the line into segments marking every seven years of your life.

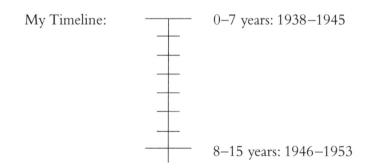

My Timeline:

0–7 years: 1938–1945

8–15 years: 1946–1953

~ *Part 1* *(30 to 40 minutes)*

On one side of the vertical line, write down the significant moments and people from each segment of your life. Begin with the obvious life cycle markers: graduations, marriages or commitments, divorces or separations, the loss of loved ones, becoming an orphan, births, adoptions, life decisions, transitions, career changes, achievements, and failures.

In a different color, add other events: accidents, abuses (including spiritual abuses), illnesses, surgeries, travels, love relationships (beginnings and endings), your first television or computer, and other events that may have precipitated ethical or spiritual insights.

Finally, choose another color and add historical events that have affected your life values: the Depression, World War II, the Holocaust, television, humans in space, assassinations, the Vietnam War, the fall of the Berlin Wall, terrorist attacks.

Set your timeline aside for at least a day. When you reread it, you may remember additional items. Include them.

~ *Part 2* *(45 to 60 minutes)*

Return to your timeline to reflect on the spiritual meaning behind the events in your life. On the other side of the vertical line – opposite each event – write brief notes indicating your feelings and insights about the meaning of these events, how they affected your life, and how they influenced your spirituality. Comment especially on those events that precipitated decisions and actions that changed the direction of your life. Use a colored pen to circle the notes most closely tied to your spiritual journey.

~ *Part 3* *(60 minutes)*

In this section, you will reflect and write on the whole of your spiritual journey. Consider:

- How has your spiritual perspective changed over time? Are these changes due to specific experiences or to your cognitive development? Write about how life experience has molded your spiritual beliefs.

This day is the culmination of years of study, of my blood pounding out a steady rhythm of longing for the Divine. Thank you for being here as witnesses. I am deeply grateful, especially for all of you who continually support me in my life and choices. I am a very lucky and blessed woman. I pray that all of you will be blessed with people to share with and support you, as I am.

Torah speaks not only about relationships through time, but also about our responsibilities across time. In his book *Of Water and the Spirit,* African shaman Malidoma Patrice Somé talks about his people's sense of time and obligation. He must redeem the actions of his ancestors. If an ancestor hurt another person, and that hurt was not resolved or healed, it is likely that Somé's life will be affected and he may be called upon to create some kind of resolution. This is a radical concept for many people.

This African tribal belief is similar to many Native American beliefs about time, responsibility, and our place on the earth. It is similar to a Jewish belief that if we fail to keep our obligations, not only will we pay, but the earth itself will become barren. The Torah can be read as an environmental codebook: The land must rest, just as we must. Fruit-bearing trees are never to be cut down in acts of war; animals are to be treated with compassion and concern. Lack of foresight, vision, and respect for our planet leads to ruin.

The Torah both cautions us and guides us. It asks us to be respectful and to let our hearts determine how we should live. If I am responsible for the mistakes and woundings of my ancestors, then I have a lot of work to do. Likewise, I reap the benefits of their goodness and grace if they were devoted to good works and loving-kindness. Conversely, if my great-great-grandchildren will be paying for my mistakes, then I really want to be careful about what I do. I want to step gently on the earth and work very hard to do no harm. My children will reap pain or grace based on my choices.

– Nicole Barchilon Frank (Shoshanah Adamah Cohen),
Gramma Minnie's great-granddaughter, from her adult
bat mitzvah ceremony

- Have you rejected any of your earlier beliefs? If so, how and when do vestiges of those beliefs show up in your life today?
- Have you reinterpreted the meanings of past events, relationships, and experiences in light of your spiritual development or maturity? How?
- Spiritual clarity often comes at midlife, after failures and defeats have dampened youthful idealism. Was there a time in your life when you experienced a spiritual low point? For many of us, times of painful reflection ultimately lead to greater self-knowledge, a kind of rebirth in which we establish a new or deeper relationship with the Divine. How has your suffering damaged or enriched your spirituality?

Be sure to share your writing with friends or the women in your legacy circle; witnessing others' significant experiences may jog your memory and help you clarify your thinking. You may wish to return to this exercise and write in greater detail about specific events, insights, or periods in your life.

Betrayal

Betrayal – by men, women, and even ourselves – activates more rage and grief than other losses. Few people can claim that they've never committed an act of betrayal; indeed, it seems an unavoidable fact of being human. But how does betrayal affect our spiritual development? Is betrayal a forgivable or unforgivable act? To explore these questions, we return to our mythic matriarch, Sarah.

Regret is an appalling waste of energy; you can't build on it; it's only good for wallowing in.
– Katherine Mansfield

REFLECTION AND WRITING
~ *Part 1*   *(10 to 20 minutes)*
Review Sarah's story on page 32, focusing specifically on the abuses and betrayals she experienced and committed. Now, imagine that you are Sarah. As

Sarah, make a list of the ways you betrayed others, acts that you may consider unforgivable. After you have made your list, read it aloud, either alone or in your legacy circle.

~ *Part 2*   *(15 to 30 minutes)*

Which of Sarah's acts remind you of things you have done – ways that you've betrayed yourself or others – that you find unforgivable? Make a list of your unforgivable acts. Write about one act from your list. How have you reconciled this act with your spiritual beliefs? How have your beliefs allowed you to find emotional closure? Repeat this exercise as many days as your list is long.

~ *Part 3*   *(30 to 60 minutes)*

Write about the effects of betrayal on your spiritual life and development. Consider:

- What do you know about your ancestors and the history of betrayal in your family? How have you been affected by a legacy of betrayal?
- Have you ever been betrayed by those from whom you expected protection? How?
- Write about ways you have betrayed yourself (for example, by failing to speak, live your truth, or use your power).

Forgiveness

Forgiveness is the key to action and freedom.
– Hannah Arendt

Some people believe that forgiveness is God's exclusive domain, that to say the words "I forgive you" is hubris of the worst kind. Others believe that we are partners with God in healing the world, that we are made in God's image and so need to be forgiving.

Everyone makes mistakes, and we need to learn tolerance for others' mistakes as well as for our own. But forgiveness must be balanced with honoring our wounds, our hurt feelings, the reality of being

I believe that even my most shameful actions are forgivable. Nevertheless, betraying my brother many years ago continues to affect my values and relationships, even now.

When I was seventeen years old, I blocked the windows in my kitchen, pushed rags under the door, opened the oven, put a pillow at its base, and turned on the gas. I lay my head on the pillow and thought, "This will serve my father right. He will be sorry when I'm dead."

Then I thought of my nine-year-old brother coming home from school and finding me. His mother dead when he was six, his sister a suicide three years later. I turned off the gas, opened the windows and doors, and resolved to leave. I'd promised myself I would stay until he was fifteen years old. Now I knew I couldn't. I abandoned him.

I've tried to make it up to him over the years, but he's broken. Drugs, alcohol, a wasted life, a wasted talent. He was my first child, the one I failed. His destruction has made me a protective mother, a woman who has tried to be the perfect mother ever since.

– Janice Maxson

neglected, abused, and betrayed. Women are usually expected to forgive, but seldom do we feel that our pain has been understood. We want to be loving, not punishing, and we want to minimize our pain. But forgiveness can't be hurried. It has its own timetable.

And what about women who cannot forgive? Many women have had unspeakable and unforgivable abuses done to them. When we have been subjected to abuse, disrespect, or degradation, we should not force ourselves to forgive. Being real with ourselves means permitting ourselves not to forgive unless and until we are ready. In "Beyond Forgiveness," Rabbi Susan Schnur explains, "It is not . . . that forgiveness is the bottom line, but rather that emotional resolution is. That is the real achievement and hard-won freedom. . . . Sometimes there is only one thing that makes forgiving possible: not forgiving. . . . Exhorting people to forgive . . . might be an important civilizing prod for men, but it's harassment for some women." What a relief to forgive ourselves for being unable to forgive others – to thereby honor our emotions, deepening and strengthening our spiritual integrity.

We often cling to old resentments, failing to forgive in the hope that something will change. One way that Twelve Step programs describe forgiveness is "letting go of the hope for a better past." Holding on to old resentments, wishing things had been different, and blaming others can be replaced by the spiritual act of accepting reality and taking responsibility for life now. This in no way absolves another person of his or her responsibility for what was done. But it does provide an opportunity to acknowledge our wounds without using our spiritual energy on self-pity, blame, or resentment. Sometimes this means forgiving another person; sometimes it means integrating the betrayal and moving on.

We must learn the art of creating boundaries that protect, nurture and sustain all we cherish.

– Sarah Ban Breathnach

To forgive is to abandon your right to pay back the perpetrator in his own coin, but it is a loss that liberates the victim.

– Archbishop Desmond Tutu

REFLECTION AND WRITING *(30 to 45 minutes)*

Make a list of the ways that Sarah suffered at the hands of others, including Abraham, Pharaoh, Hagar, Ishmael, Isaac, and God. Which, if any, of these acts do you think are unforgivable? Next, list the hurtful things that have been done to you, acts that you have been unable to forgive. Write about one of these acts. Was this an unforgivable act, or one that you have not yet forgiven? Take as many days as you need to write about the other acts on your list.

Making and Seeking Amends

Twelve Step programs encourage us to practice self-care and healthy relationships as part of our spiritual journey. The Eighth Step says, "Make a list of all persons we have harmed, and become willing to make amends to them all." This is followed by the Ninth Step, "Make direct amends to such people wherever possible, except when to do so would injure them or others." Both steps respect a timetable that is often beyond human understanding. The slogan "Progress, not perfection" can help combat our impatience over the snail-slow pace of forgiveness.

Forgiving can take time. It takes as long as it takes, and it's important to have patience with yourself and your internal process.
— Denise Linn

Living in turbulent times, we're more aware of our mortality than ever, and none of us knows how long she will live. This uncertainty leads many women to ask forgiveness for the harm they've caused — and to consider forgiving those who have harmed them.

REFLECTION AND WRITING *(30 to 60 minutes)*

List those people to whom you want to offer amends or forgiveness, including yourself. Next to each person's name, write a short description of the harm that was done. Now, choose one person from your list. Write about your reasons for seeking resolution, and consider how you might do it (face to face, in writing, or silently in your heart). Repeat this exercise as many times as you wish.

Ritual, Prayer, and Meditation

Get in touch with the still small voice inside you. That voice is steady and clear and you can trust it and use it as your guide all your life.
– Sharon Strassfeld

Rituals evoke a commitment of the heart.
– Marianne Williamson

Like beads strung along a thread, the events of our life contain meaning for us.
– Manuela Dunn Mascetti and Priya Hemenway

Prayer and ritual are vehicles for expressing our love, respect, and awe. They elevate the everyday to the sacred, bringing us closer to the Divine. But for many women, traditional prayers and rituals simply don't resonate. Some women feel alienated: Most rituals, created by men, endow God with a masculine identity. Women are banned from full participation in certain religious rituals. Few religions have educated us about the value of rituals or encouraged us to develop prayers and ceremonies that serve our own needs. For some women, rote memorization has stripped prayer and ritual of their meaning. For these and other reasons, many women have discarded traditional rituals, which often leaves them aching for spiritual connection.

Women need to reclaim this connection, seeking out rituals that are meaningful and satisfying, rituals that feel like home. For some women this means a return – with mature understanding – to the rituals of their childhood faiths. For others it is the discovery of ancient women's practices. Still other women create their own prayers and rituals that meet their specific needs.

As you embark on this leg of your spiritual journey, do not allow yourself to be seduced by the repetition and familiarity of other people's rituals. Think about the meaning behind each ritual, decide if it fits you, and, if not, let it go. If a ritual is to maintain its meaning, we must continue to breathe life into it, keeping it and ourselves vital and real.

You may wish to explore or create rituals involving candles, incense, oils, chanting, drumming, meditation, or prayer. For many people, prayer beads play a particularly significant role in their relationship with the Divine. In their book *Prayer Beads,* authors Manuela Dunn Mascetti and Priya Hemenway note that "the bead was first recognized thousands of years ago, by the very earliest of humans, as an object that had a very special relationship with the world of the

I pray that I can do something worthy each day
To lighten the load of others,
To contribute to freedom.
I must remain conscious enough to remember
That balance gives me strength
For informed choices and proaction.

God, hear me, help me not to hate,
Free me from the bondage hate produces.
Keep my runway steadied by faith.
There is no other landing place for my fear,
For to trip into the hole of immobilizing depression,
Selective denial, or chosen passivity
Would take my soul, and they cannot have it.

– adapted from "I Hope I Don't Trip," by Ethelyn Cohen

spirit. . . . Whether made of seed, nut, shell, bone, wood, gem, or glass, beads were worn because they were felt to contain some mysterious link between the world we can see and the world we cannot."

Similarly, writing your own prayers may bring you closer to the Divine. It is an opportunity to honor the Creator, express gratitude for abundance, communicate your daily concerns, even address the darker side of your nature or the world. For example, "God, remind me each day that these precious children are so different from each other and from me. You created them to be unique. Show me how to love each of them just the way they need to be loved. Give me discernment to understand their needs."

Meditation can also open doors to the sacred. As Mother Teresa said, "God is the friend of silence." But for many women, the thought of seeking silence to empty one's mind is a source of tremendous anxiety. Women tend to survive in the world by multitasking. We occupy our minds and hands in part to avoid asking life's deepest questions. But for those who can risk the silence, there are many forms of meditation, including sitting meditations, walking meditations, yoga, and tai chi. Some women practice mindfulness in their daily activities, while others find spiritual connection in nature. Still other women enjoy the meditative benefits of the labyrinth. Dating back to the Bronze Age, the labyrinth, symbolizing death and rebirth, has been used as a meditative structure. In recent decades, labyrinths have enjoyed renewed interest throughout the Western world. The famous labyrinth etched into the floor of the cathedral at Chartres has been reproduced in many cities, spiritual retreat centers, college campuses, and social halls.

Spiritual communities are yet another form of religious expression. According to Dr. Jean Shinoda Bolen, author of *The Millionth Circle*, women are creating spiritual communities all over the world, coming together to practice both ancient and modern sacred traditions. One such community, The Women's Well in Concord, Massachusetts, offers

Washing the dishes is like bathing a baby Buddha. The profane is sacred. Everyday mind is Buddha's mind.
– Thich Nhat Hanh

While our speed may keep us safe, it also keeps us malnourished. It prevents us from tasting those things that would truly make us safe. Prayer, touch, kindness, fragrance – all these things that live in rest, and not in speed.
– Wayne Muller

Looking back on my life I wonder why
I did so many foolish things.
How could I have been so careless
to ignore the warning signs,
turns that would lead me to disaster?
Recklessly I plunged into danger.

In retrospect
maybe those turns were needed
to get me where I am today.
Now I have reached the center
the place of wholeness and enlightenment.
But only for a moment can I stay.
Then back again into the turns and twists
of unexpected detours.
The maze of life will lead to new surprises.

> – from "Grace Cathedral," by Eve Hearst,
> written after walking the labyrinth

programs inspired by Hallie Iglehart Austen, author of *The Heart of the Goddess.* She writes: "We must bring back the power of women's wisdom. This strength is not a power over anything else, but a force emanating from deep within each of us." Anne Yeomans, cofounder of The Women's Well, notes that their community "contributes to the healing and empowerment of women; its purpose is to honor the feminine in a world out of balance."

REFLECTION AND WRITING

~ *Part 1*   *(20 to 30 minutes)*

List the issues and concerns you would like to discuss with the God of your understanding. Choose one topic. Try saying or writing your own prayer about this topic, then sit quietly and listen for a response. Even if you don't get an answer, you will be amazed at how satisfying it is to express your concerns in this way. You may want to return to this exercise and write special prayers for several areas of your life.

~ *Part 2*   *(10 to 60 minutes)*

Today, women are not only transforming traditional rituals, but creating new ones that show reverence for the earth and all of life. Write about your sacred rituals and how they've affected your spirituality. Consider the following:

- How did you experience rituals as a child, an adolescent, a young woman? Your exploration may take you back to a place of chanting or singing, a time when your heart was open and music transported you. Consider the risks and benefits of practicing rituals from your former or current faith tradition.

- Which rituals do you practice alone? Which do you practice with others? Did you create these rituals or are they a part of your faith tradition? Write about paths to wholeness, community, and relationship with the Divine.

- What rituals have you created for daily life? For special times? Write about the components of your life for which you'd like to create rituals.
- How do listening, meditating, walking, or praying play a role in your spiritual life? Write about music and other aspects of your rituals that are beyond words.
- How do you silence your mind to connect with the Divine? How do you find a quiet space for your rituals? How have rituals helped you to experience your life with gratitude? How have they connected you with the sacred?

Celebration

Before we move on to writing our legacies, we will take a moment to appreciate all that we are – mothers, lovers, creators, protectors, warriors, and peacemakers – and to celebrate our ever-evolving spirituality.

Of course, many women are more comfortable accepting criticisms than compliments. If this sounds like you, be prepared to silence your inner critic, celebrate your life, and share its sacredness with the world.

I never thought that money or fine clothes would make you happy. My concept of happiness is to be fulfilled spiritually.
– Coretta Scott King

REFLECTION AND WRITING

~ *Part 1* (20 to 30 minutes)

Complete the following sentences, reflecting on the spiritual aspect of each topic. When you have finished, feel free to add sentences of your own. You may want to include lessons you have learned, pain you have suffered, difficulties you have survived, and experiences of wholeness and spiritual connection. If you wish, you may expand on any of these topics.

- What I appreciate about my spiritual self includes . . .
- What I especially love about my life today is . . .
- I feel blessed as a woman because . . .

- Things I love about being a mother are . . .
- What's wonderful about being a lover is . . .
- What I celebrate about being a friend is . . .
- What I take the greatest joy in is . . .
- Things that I do to celebrate my life include . . .

~ *Part 2*   *(30 to 60 minutes)*

Review your responses in part 1 to determine your deepest-held values. Create a prayer, song, or ritual to celebrate any of these values.

~

I have met brave women who are exploring the outer edge of human possibility, with no history to guide them, and with a courage to make themselves vulnerable that I find moving beyond words.
– Gloria Steinem

Celebration, divine connection, prayers for loved ones, taking responsibility for our earth and for the well-being of our great-great-grandchildren – each of these acts bears witness to the depth of our spirituality. We are spiritual beings, continuously growing and developing as we journey through our lives, one day at a time.

"To be rooted is perhaps the most important and least recognized need of the human soul. To be able to give, one has to possess, and we possess no other life, no other living sap, than the treasures stored up from our past and digested, assimilated and created afresh by us," writes Simone Weil. To give yourself the fullest sense of what you possess – the treasures of your history and life experience – review all the writings you have filed away so far. Gather your sense of self, and know how much you are blessed.

You are now prepared to focus on your legacy for future generations. You are ready to create your spiritual-ethical will.

Documenting a legacy – creating a spiritual-ethical will – is the last leg of our sacred journey. In the chapters that follow, you will transform the legacies of the present and past into gifts for future generations. You will articulate your values, your wisdom, your sincerest hopes for loved ones. You'll decide which of your valuable possessions to bequeath, how to distribute your financial legacy, and how you hope to be remembered. Finally, you'll explore alternative legacies: contributions to art, nature, and community.

At the end of this section, you will review all of your work and determine which writings to include in your spiritual-ethical will. Chapter 12 offers simple tips for editing, preserving, and presenting your document to loved ones.

Let us now take this long-anticipated step toward the future, linking ourselves to family, community, and generations to come.

May you experience gratitude for your abundant blessings.
May your writing flow easily and elegantly. May your stories, values,
and wisdom live on as enduring gifts to future generations.

PART THREE

The Future ~

~

May your values, memories,
and life experience become
the wisdom by which you
bless the future.

~

CHAPTER EIGHT

Sharing Your Values and Blessings

Each of us has been blessed with abundance in our lives. Consequently, we may feel enormous gratitude not only for the gifts we've received, but for the women we've become – strong, wise, and creative women with layers of rich life experience. Our task, as legacy writers, is to determine what we value most in life, then convey these values to our descendants. In so doing, we maintain important traditions within our families and communities.

Marcia Falk writes that "tradition is not just what we inherit from the past; it is also what we create and pass on to the future. Tradition necessarily implies process, the continual forging of links on an unending chain." We are the links between the past and the future, receiving our ancestors' values and handing them down with our own.

My Core Values

In our every deliberation, we must consider the impact of our decisions on the next seven generations.

– From the Great Law of the Iroquois Confederacy

In order to leave a legacy that matters, we need to know what we value in life. Integrity, optimism, compassion, self-sufficiency, courage, creativity, honesty – your list of values may be long indeed. Values are principles to which we are committed, characteristics that we admire, or vows that we strive to uphold. Some values have been a part of us since childhood; others have arisen out of life experiences and influential relationships.

But values also include the things we love most about our lives – a good book, coffee on the porch, a raucous family get-together, an intimate conversation, playing with our grandchildren. These make our lives worth living, and it is our love of life that we want to communicate in our legacies.

REFLECTION AND WRITING *(30 minutes)*

Reflect on your values, on what really matters to you. Consider every significant aspect of your life, including:

- Family, tribe, history, tradition
- Religion, spirituality, faith, prayer, purpose
- Education, learning, study
- Relationships, respect for life
- Work, career, vocation, mission
- Culture, beauty, art, literature, music, sport
- Giving, generosity, service
- Hopes, dreams, vision, meaning

Now, take a fresh sheet of paper and title it "What's Most Important to Me." Write as many short sentences as you have thoughts. For example, "One thing that gives me pleasure is hearing my granddaughter's sweet voice calling me

'Granny.' " Or, "I am committed to combating racist attitudes wherever I find them, even within me."

Write quickly, without priority, to capture all your values and everything you love about your life. Use any of these prompts:

- I value . . .
- I believe that . . .
- I believe in . . .
- I am committed to . . .
- What matters most in life is . . .
- I am blessed with . . .
- I am grateful for . . .
- One thing that gives me pleasure is . . .

You may add to this list at any time. You've probably found that sleeping on an idea or sharing it with your legacy circle will further stimulate your thoughts. But for now, let this exercise rest so you can move on to the next topic.

Living My Values

Our values, principles, and beliefs are most clearly demonstrated in the way we live our lives. A woman who is proud to support her family demonstrates strength, courage, and creativity. Women who recycle, advocate nonviolence, or donate their time or money to charity exemplify compassion and service.

In this exercise you will explore your many positive actions and qualities, a healing antidote to the inner critic that we all have and hear from regularly. Once you've articulated your values and how you demonstrate them in your daily life, you can decide how to share your values as part of your legacy.

We must be sure to tell our children about the goodness of people, to express again and again ... that our individual acts of kindness make a difference.

– Anne Roiphe

REFLECTION AND WRITING

~ *Part 1* (15 minutes)

Reflect on the many things you have done in your life that you are proud of, significant things and everyday things. Make a list, numbering from 1 to 30 on a fresh sheet of paper. It may be slow going at first, but once you start, you will have much to say. List everything you can think of without making value judgments. Begin each entry with one of these phrases:

- I am proud that . . .
- I am proud of myself for . . .
- I feel proud of myself as a . . .
- I feel most proud of myself when I . . .

Here is an excerpt from my own list:

I am proud of my volunteer work reading for the blind.

I am proud of myself for repairing a dripping pipe under my kitchen sink.

I am proud of myself for creating a ritual ceremony to begin anew after my divorce.

I am proud that I learned how to program my VCR.

I am proud of serving in the Peace Corps.

I am proud that I exercise four times a week.

I am proud of my efforts to connect with my heritage and learn about its traditions.

If you are working in a legacy circle, go around the circle sharing one thing you are proud of. Continue around the circle until everyone has shared as many items as they choose. Remember that you have the right to pass. If you hear something that sparks an idea, add another line to your list.

~ *Part 2* (10 to 20 minutes)

Choose one item from your list and write about it in more detail. What, specifically, makes you proud? Consider the significance or symbolic meaning of your action. You may repeat this exercise daily, writing on the same topic or on several different topics.

~ *Part 3* (15 minutes)

Now that you've written about one or more topics, return to your original list. Next to each statement, write down the values illustrated. If you are working in a legacy circle, you can assist each other in naming these values. For example:

I am proud of my volunteer work reading for the blind: *passion and service.*

I am proud of myself for repairing a dripping pipe under my kitchen sink: *logic and independence.*

I am proud of myself for creating a ritual ceremony to begin anew after my divorce: *creativity and self-care.*

I am proud that I learned how to program my VCR: *initiative and courage.*

I am proud of serving in the Peace Corps: *service and generosity.*

I am proud that I exercise four times a week: *perseverance.*

I am proud of my effort to connect with my heritage and to learn about its traditions: *curiosity, open-mindedness, faith, and belonging.*

Take a few minutes to reflect on the influence your principles and values have had on your life. Write down insights, especially those that surprised you. Then, file this exercise with your other writings.

My Most Valuable Possessions

If values are the foundation of your legacy, then tangibles – money, material items, and your spiritual-ethical will – are the bricks. Chances are, your most valued possessions are those that link you to your history. They commemorate special times and occasions, or they've been passed down as family heirlooms. Some are mementos from the past. Others may be your own creations – a quilt, a painting, a carving.

One of my most prized possessions is a glass vase that wouldn't fetch 50 cents at a garage sale.
– Anonymous

To keep a lamp burning we have to keep putting oil in it.
— Mother Teresa

To ensure that future generations receive something even more meaningful than a serving tray or grandmother clock, use your spiritual-ethical will to document what these objects represent to you. Should you fail to communicate the meanings attached to your most beloved possessions, one day both the items and their significance will be lost at the inevitable garage sale.

REFLECTION AND WRITING *(10 to 20 minutes)*

List your possessions that have value beyond their material worth, those beloved items that you want to pass on as part of your legacy. You might ask friends, family, children, and grandchildren if any of your possessions are especially meaningful to them. Add these to your list.

Evaluate each object on your list to determine how it relates to your values. To plumb an item's meaning, write about the object over the course of several days, no more than ten to twenty minutes per day. If the history of the object has been lost, you might consider writing from your midrashic imagination (see chapter 2). Here are some prompts to help you get started:

- Where did this item come from? How did it come to you?
- What is the history of this item? What is the story behind this object that makes it valuable? What does it represent for you?
- To whom will you give this item? Why? What do you want this person to know about it?

If you include this writing in your spiritual-ethical will, indicate where the object is and when you want the recipient to receive it. You might also tag the object in an inconspicuous place with the name of the recipient.

Day 1

To my granddaughters, Sophie, Lily, and Grace,

My Gramma Rosa brought these candlesticks with her from Kovno in 1906. They have meant a great deal to me.

Some years ago, my male rabbi suggested to me that women should light Shabbat candles because "God commanded it." After a lifetime of disdain for authority, I committed to experiment with consciously doing an act because God commanded it, to explore the idea that there really is a deity, a divine source, a force that has more power, more authority, than I do. This was the beginning of my relationship with God and Judaism.

Each time I light the candles in the Friday twilight, I begin my prayer by thanking God for giving me, a woman, the responsibility of welcoming, birthing, the holiest of Jewish traditions: Shabbat. I often feel, as I light the candles in my Gramma Rosa's candlesticks, that I am part of a community of women throughout time and around the globe. As each welcomes Shabbat with her candle lighting, she recreates a partnership with God and the human community.

I bequeath this tradition to you, my granddaughters, along with Gramma Rosa's candlesticks. I also bequeath these writings, done over the course of several days, in the hope that you will experience your history and feel a connection to your great-great-grandmother, who immigrated to America from Russia. Please pass the candlesticks and this writing on to whomever carries my name after I am gone.

– Love, Granny Rachael

Day 2

Dear Rachael,

When I left Kovno to come to America, I only had one valise, shabby and dark. In it I packed my responsibility as a Jewish woman, my brass candlesticks, so I could make Shabbos in the new world. No matter how different a place this new home might be, no matter where I would go in the world, I could count on the fact that there would be Shabbos, and I would welcome it in, praying to bring its powerful light to my family and to the world.

Where did I get those candlesticks? My mother, bless her soul, gave them to me when I was thirteen – a birthday gift, and a sign that I was now mature enough to take on the responsibility of a Jewish woman. She had commissioned the brazier near our home in Kiev to make them for me. It was a surprise, and I know that she saved her kopeks for many months to be able to pay him.

These candlesticks were the very first thing I packed. It was like carrying all I knew of my mother – of her love for me and for our tradition.

Each Friday, when I lit my candles and welcomed Shabbos into our home, I felt my mother's presence. These candlesticks were her legacy to me. They were my connection to my family and to all Jewish families who welcome Shabbos with God's gift of fire.

– Love, Rosa

Day 3

The image of Gramma Rosa's suitcase calls up a powerful memory for me: the battered suitcases in a pile outside a cattle car, that horrifyingly real "prop" in Washington's Holocaust Museum. How strongly I felt the pain of hope followed by betrayal. I imagined people being forced to pack all that mattered to them in one suitcase. I heard the finality of the doors slamming shut, the creak of the wheels on the track, the cries of children sucking for air as the train packed full of people headed for. . . .

What to carry, what to leave? Practical thoughts about what would be needed where they were going. And the horrific irony, that where they were going required no packing. No wonder they packed; no wonder they had hope. Who could have known they'd be forced onto trains packed fuller than the suitcases left behind on the platform? Who could have believed they were being sent to their deaths?

They, like Gramma Rosa, packed what mattered most, what would be indispensable wherever they debarked. I wonder how many pairs of candlesticks were packed.

Day 4

Gramma Rosa died before I was born. As I try to get a better sense of who she was, I keep returning to that suitcase. What else did she pack? Maybe her favorite kneading bowl? Did my father come home after school on Fridays and smell challah baking, signaling the coming of Shabbat? Or was Gramma Rosa out making sure that the more recent immigrants had enough to make Shabbos? I see her purposeful stride, her black lace-up boots (scuffed but well made, a gift from her introverted husband, a watchmaker), taking her intense energy away from the house so her husband could repair watches in peace. But he was proud of her, of her straight back, her sure manner, the powerful ethic of *tikkun olam* (repairing our broken world) driving her every day.

It didn't take her long to find her way around, to let the butcher know when he was charging too much, to remind the more fortunate of their obligations to the newcomers. If you didn't want to be harassed you turned the other way when you saw her coming, or you reached into your pocket to give her a few coins for *tzedakah*.

She was intense; she would be neither ignored nor denied. She was tough. Had she lived in a slightly different time or place she would have joined with other women, demanding better labor conditions, saving children from sweatshops, even running for office – a model for Bella Abzug. But here she was, in Minneapolis.

I see her marching up the steps of a school building in 1920 for the first election in which women could vote. With tears in her eyes, awe in her throat, and pride in her heart, she thanked God that her children weren't in Russia. And she felt deep sadness that her mother, Beyla Brodsky, couldn't see her vote in the United States of America.

Day 5

Rosa, you had a passion for life, you cared deeply about people. You were head- and heart-strong, sensuous, undaunted by Cossacks, by czars, by dogma, or by your mother's old-fashioned hold on tradition.

When I think of you I see a body and a face that mean business, a woman not easily swayed, one who rejects others' opinions. What made her so hard? Was it betrayal and pain? Was it adherence to an inner voice of duty, responsibility? What drove her? Those are legitimate questions, but ones I can only speculate about. I wish I had known you, Gramma Rosa. I wish I knew what your real legacy was to me.

Day 6

Dear Ra-che-le:

I never knew you, but I dreamed your birth and I see you walking the earth after me. When I died, I had no grandchildren. Ethel was briefly married then divorced, and Benny seemed more interested in playing around with his friends than settling down to be a husband and a father. He seemed a lost soul and still a boy. But I hoped, especially as I lay dying of pneumonia, that one day there would be a Ra-che-le who would keep my memory alive and carry my energy forward.

At the turn of the century I was a young woman, hopeful and idealistic. I saw progress for women and children in my lifetime, but the work is far from done. I bequeath you this unfinished work to make the world a better place. Never forget those who have less than you, and never forget those who look like they have more than you but don't feed their souls. Though you won't know it for a long time, your job, like mine was, will be to help feed people's souls as well as their stomachs.

Heed this old wisdom well, Ra-che-le, my dear granddaughter: the work is far bigger than you, but you must never let that deter you from persevering and doing your part. It is your job to discover what your part is and then to do it, never questioning that you are doing what our God wants you to do.

What else do I bequeath you? My candlesticks, which I wrapped in my best dress and packed in the valise I brought to the new country. Light those candles – to remember me, and to remember the importance of family, of Shabbos. The light symbolizes our responsibility to bring more light into the world.

Finally, I bequeath you my smile, which many have also called light. I read that Florence Nightingale could ignite the light of hope and the healing power of love with her smile. You will have my smile, and more. That smile will endear you to people, and they will give you their trust. Do your best not to betray it.

I eagerly await seeing you and loving you as you love your children and grandchildren.

– Ra-che-le, bat Joseph and Beyla

Blessing Future Generations

Somewhere between the third and sixth centuries C.E., the ethical will came to be used as a pedagogic tool encouraging men to pass on moral and ethical instructions to their sons. The Talmud is clear, stating that every man is responsible for teaching his sons to study Torah, learn a trade, and learn to swim. Aside from the layers of metaphoric meaning in these instructions, we might notice similarities in the directions we received from our own families: be good, work hard, take care of yourself and your family.

In 1916, one of the great ethical wills in history, written by Sholem Aleichem, was read into the Congressional Record and published in the *New York Times*. In the tenth and final paragraph, he wrote to his children, "Take good care of your mother, beautify her old age, sweeten her bitter life, heal her broken heart." Some people regard this as an admission of failure in Sholem Aleichem's relationship with his wife. His words, they argue, transfer responsibility for her happiness to their children. At the very least, his instructions seem an unfair and impossible burden as well as a patriarchal demand. If he meant to convey respect, love, and caring as a way to honor their mother, he might have used a different style to deliver this message. Here are his instructions written as a blessing: "May you continue to be blessed by the presence of your mother in your lives, by her love for you, and by your generosity toward her."

While it may be easier to communicate our values as instructions, many women don't want to tell loved ones how to live. Blessing loved ones, however – with our love, our values, our hopes for their future – is a less intrusive way of sharing our deepest selves. By transforming our instructions into blessings, we offer our wisdom and experience without attempting to control our loved ones' lives.

May God keep you safe 'til the word of your life is fully spoken.
– Irish blessing

We transmit our wisdom to future generations. This process not only seeds the future, but crowns an Elder's life with worth and nobility.
– Rabbi Zalman Schachter-Shalomi

REFLECTION AND WRITING

~ *Part 1*   *(15 to 30 minutes)*

List the instructions you received from your family, community, and religion. Consider those that were clearly communicated as well as those that were expressed indirectly.

Now, make a list of instructions you want to leave for future generations. These may be similar to or very different from the instructions you were given. Jot down as many thoughts as you can. When you're finished, narrow your list to the three most essential instructions. Write these as brief phrases. For example: Be generous. Love deeply. Listen to nature.

~ *Part 2*   *(30 to 60 minutes)*

Choose one of your instructions and write it at the top of a fresh sheet of paper. Then, write it as a blessing. Getting started may be the most difficult part of this exercise, because most of us are unpracticed in thinking and writing in the form of blessings. Here are some opening words to help you begin:

- May you always . . .
- May you be blessed as I have been with . . .
- May God (or your higher power) grant you . . .

You may need to write several drafts of your blessing before it feels right to you. Read each draft aloud. How does it sound? What do you think about its tone? Do the words convey your message? Have you written a blessing or a command? How do you think the recipient might respond? When you are satisfied with this blessing, move on to your other essential instructions. Convert these into blessings, too.

To many women, blessings feel honest, gentle, and personal – more like gifts than instructions, which seem a distinctly masculine form of legacy writing. Some women, however, regard blessings as an indirect, seductive, manipulative style of trying to control the future. Clearly, blessings won't resonate with everyone. But if you are moved by the spiritual integrity of blessings, you may find yourself using them frequently as you document your legacy.

Instruction: Take care of the earth – be in awe of it; it is a magnificent creation.

Blessing: May your life be blessed by the scent of a flower, the whisper of the wind, the quiet of a sunset, and the movement of gentle waters.

– Sandy Baines

Instruction: Always give away a percentage of your time, talent, and money.

Blessing: May you always be blessed with enough time, talent, and money to share generously with your community.

– Deborah Levin Stillman

Instruction: Laugh at yourself; it will soothe you.

Blessing: May you always be blessed with laughter.

– Letitia Zilar

Instruction: Love others.

Blessing: I bless you with eyes, ears, and heart to recognize and appreciate love in all its forms and to give it generously and without regard.

– Dona Billey-Weiler

Instruction: Love deeply.

Blessing: May you be blessed as I have been with people to love deeply, and may your love be returned in abundance.

– Judy Hostnick

Instruction: Take time for quiet and solitude every day.

Blessing: May your life be blessed with times of solitude and places of beauty to nurture your spirit, so that you may bring forth your own gifts into the world.

– Bev Harries

Some women include individual blessings for each child and grandchild as part of their spiritual-ethical wills. Others write special blessings for family occasions. By reading our blessings aloud, we ritualize, affirm, and make sacred our relationships. Once you get a feel for them, blessings may become a satisfying method of communicating your deepest thoughts and feelings to those you love – and imparting your values and wisdom in your spiritual-ethical will.

Before you move on to the next section, take time to record your thoughts about writing blessings.

Bestowing My Wisdom

The best lives and stories are made up of minute particulars that somehow are also universal and of use to others as well as oneself.
– Barbara Myerhoff

Like all heroines, we have had life lessons to learn. We have slain our dragons and wrestled with our angels. We have returned, limping, from those dark nights of the soul, those mythic battles, and found ourselves whole and new. Through our suffering we have acquired a gift more precious than knowledge, more vital than understanding. We have gained wisdom. To clarify how experience becomes wisdom, we return to our now familiar friend, Sarah of Genesis – prototypic pioneer, immigrant, mother, and friend.

REFLECTION AND WRITING

~ *Part 1*   *(20 minutes)*

After reviewing Sarah's story on page 32, reflect on the lessons life taught her. Jot down notes – key words or short phrases – or make a list of what you think she learned from her experiences.

~ *Part 2*   *(30 to 60 minutes)*

Consider which of Sarah's lessons you, too, have learned from experience. Though the lessons may be similar, your experiences may be quite different.

Some of your learning has been simple and pain free, but some lessons may have included great suffering, grief, and loss.

For a thorough review, you might reflect on your writings from chapters 5 and 6 and your spiritual timeline from chapter 7. Where have you succeeded in life? Where have you failed? What have you learned from your successes and failures? Make a list of your life lessons.

~ *Part 3*   *(10 minutes)*

In this step you will express your wisdom to future generations by creating a pithy maxim, your own personal proverb. Choose one of your life lessons, then take no more than ten minutes to hone and polish the words that express your learning. This is a good time to consult your thesaurus.

Write a clear and concise statement of your wisdom. You may decide to capture each of your life lessons in one pithy statement. Here are some of Sarah's, as written by women in legacy circles:

> Faith is waiting patiently for God to act.
> Trust your higher power.
> The selfish path does not lead to truth.
> Preempting God produces contrary results.
> When God is male, male is God.

~ *Part 4*   *(30 to 40 minutes)*

Now, write more fully about how you came to this wisdom. Tell the story behind it, describing the experience in which you confronted your lesson. Write about what you learned and how your experience changed your life.

This is deep material, and it would be easier to hide behind a homily. But writing from your heart is more effective than a lecture. Future generations will appreciate really knowing you, and they'll be more likely to accept your wisdom when they understand the source of your learning.

This writing integrates the wise with the personal. You may write about as many lessons as you choose to include in your spiritual-ethical will.

Honoring the Dead Honors Life

To my daughters and granddaughters:

I first tasted Millie's kugel at the meal following my mother's funeral on October 13, 1972. How well I remember that day – radiant sunshine and fluorescent yellow leaves clothed the triple-trunk birch tree at 11903 Hilloway Road.

Led by Aunt Millie, my mother's friends had arrived the day before – a swarming, loving cadre of women armed with coffeepots and serving trays. They'd checked my cupboards and refrigerator, making lists of what was needed. I had stood limp and helpless at the edge of my kitchen while they organized for shiva.

Aunt Millie, not really my aunt but a close family friend, was one of my mother's many female friends who loved me. She was affectionate, playful, cheerful, free-spirited. She often swore and broke other rules of the day about being ladylike.

I have spotty recall of those days in 1972, mostly because of the shock and numbness of early, unexpected grief. I waded through the minutes and hours as through a thick shroud of mist.

On Saturday, my father told me he hadn't known what to do, so he'd taken Mother to the hospital. On Monday an arrest. Paddled back to life? Coma, high fever, strong antibiotics, kidney malfunction. Then at dusk on Wednesday, a resident, hiding an autopsy permission form on a clipboard behind his back, took us to an airless space behind an elevator and pronounced my mother dead. I was a month short of turning thirty-five, and Mother was two weeks short of fifty-seven. And she was dead.

I remember little of the funeral. I had explained to Sid, who was almost five, that he wouldn't see Gramma Bea because her body would be in a covered box. As we sat in front of the coffin, he whispered, "Where's the box?" and I realized I'd been vague in describing its shape and size. Maybe he was expecting to see a matchbox, a cereal box, a shoe box. I had to suppress an urge to laugh aloud.

Coming back from the cemetery was a shock. In my absence, the warrior women had transformed my living room with tables set for forty or fifty people, heavily laden with the traditional postfuneral meal: hard-boiled eggs, bagels and cream cheese, tuna salad, cottage cheese, herring, and Aunt Millie's kugel.

The kugel was such a comfort as it went down – sweet and warm and solid – just what I needed to fortify me for the coming days when I would have to integrate this new reality: I no longer had a mother.

I took great comfort in the power of shiva, in the many people who came to express their condolences and tell stories. They shared their version of Bea, Auntie Bea, gifting me with aspects of her I'd not known and loving her in ways impossible for me to have imagined. I found solace in the power of a community sitting down to eat together after a burial, sharing foods symbolic of life. And I was strengthened by the power of women taking charge at a time of death – organizing, preparing, and serving food to mourners, nourishing bodies and spirits as a team of life-keepers.

As I have aged and taken my turn as a warrior woman, I have always volunteered to make the kugel, Aunt Millie's kugel. It is a tradition that keeps my memories – of my mother, her death, and her generation – alive. And it is a link to our tradition, binding us through death and life, generation to generation.

So I pass this kugel recipe down to you, my daughters and granddaughters, as part of my legacy. May you make this kugel when you become part of the cadre of women honoring the life of a beloved person who has died. Let it bring warm and solid sustenance to the survivors, helping them to mourn so they can return to life.

May Aunt Millie's kugel sweeten your lives and the lives of those you love.

NOODLE KUGEL *(In the words of Aunt Millie, October 1972)*

1 lb. wide egg noodles (boil according to directions; rinse with cold water)

Add:
- 1 quart buttermilk
- $\frac{1}{4}$ lb. melted butter or margarine
- $\frac{1}{2}$ C. sugar
- Salt – "How much? A nice teaspoonful"
- 6 eggs (well beaten)

Throw all together – eggs last – sprinkle $\frac{1}{2}$ C. Parmesan cheese on top.
Bake in 350° oven for 1 to $1\frac{1}{2}$ hours.

*May your generosity bless
all those who receive your
financial legacy.*

CHAPTER NINE

$\mathcal{F}$inancial Legacies

Given the norms of our patriarchal culture, it's not surprising that many people think a woman's wealth lies in her heart and not her checkbook. We can give our sweat and tears, our time and effort, our mothering of the world. But our money?

Women control 54 percent of the money in the United States, and, as of the new millennium, there were 6.2 million female business owners in America. Women handle money every day, earning, spending, saving, and giving. Yet when it comes to financial decisions, too many women feel disenfranchised, especially if they have never been the primary or even secondary wage earners in their families. For them, the subject of money is uncomfortable, if not terrifying.

If you're accustomed to letting your spouse or partner handle your finances, you may be tempted to skip this chapter. But take note: Life spans indicate that seven out of eight women will be widowed. This means that your finances will likely become your responsibility. And whether you have $100 or $1,000,000, your legacy will be incomplete unless you decide how your money will be used when you are gone.

In the following pages we will challenge outdated social taboos related to women and finance. You'll explore your own relationship with money, identifying your attitudes and building self-confidence. Finally, you will plan your financial legacy, determining how much money you need for your future, how much to leave to your heirs, and how much to contribute toward building a better world.

Women and Money

Esther Berger, a former PaineWebber vice president, observes that women's interest in money has been consistently discouraged, if not virtually disallowed, throughout history. "For centuries, at every turn and at every level, men made the money, and those who made it were permitted to own and control it. . . . [T]he deep-rooted presumption of masculine authority over money continues to hold women back and keep them afraid: afraid of earning money; afraid of understanding it; afraid, even, of confronting their fear of it. . . . [T]here is [also] the matter of money's perceived inelegance, a holdover from the days when the mere mention of money was considered bad form in polite circles" (*Newsweek,* 12 March 1990).

Some women do not relate to this discomfort with money. These women control their finances and have negotiated mutually respectful financial relationships with their partners. They take pride in earning, saving, spending, and donating as they see fit, confident in their ability to handle money and to support themselves and their families.

Most women, however, have a certain amount of anxiety, fear, or disinterest related to money. For many of us, even talking about money seems taboo. Perhaps we've been told throughout our lives that money is too complex for women to understand. Maybe somewhere deep inside we believe that a handsome prince will sweep us away in

Taking control of our money – being responsible for it, understanding its preciousness – is the next macro move for women.
– Frances Lear

Money you have beyond what you need for survival is either bondage or freedom.
– Mitchell Chefitz

his fancy convertible and take care of our financial needs forever. Too many of us have handed our power to a husband or partner, whether freely or under pressure, because we've never been taught otherwise.

We have found our voices in many areas of our lives. In this chapter, we work toward gaining power over our finances as well, examining our relationship with money and challenging uncomfortable perspectives.

The myth of money, of course, is that women don't know how to handle it, as if money had a gender.
– Frances Lear

REFLECTION AND WRITING

This exercise will help you identify your attitudes about finances. If you can, let go of the anxiety that may be your companion and replace it with a sense of objectivity, even playfulness. Most of us begin with deficits (pardon the pun) in this arena; some we are aware of and others we are not.

~ *Part 1*   (10 to 15 minutes)

On page 162 you'll find a list of words that refer to money. Circle three words that describe your positive relationship with money. Next, underline three words that describe negative aspects of your relationship with money. Finally, place a check mark next to three words that you wish described your relationship with money. If you think of a word not on the list that falls into one of these categories, add it.

Read your lists aloud. If you are working in a legacy circle, go around the circle and share your lists of three, noticing the commonality of attitudes that you hear. Remember that every woman has the freedom to pass.

~ *Part 2*   (20 to 30 minutes)

Write about your habits and attitudes related to earning, saving, spending, and giving. Consider the following:

* Return to your lists in part 1. How do the words in each list relate to your financial attitudes and habits?
* Are you satisfied or discouraged with your saving pattern? With your spending behaviors?

Acquisitive	Covetous	Indebted	Prudent
Affluent	Economical	Irresponsible	Responsible
Afraid	Empowered	Knowledgeable	Rich
Anxious	Envious	Lavish	Self-indulgent
Appreciative	Foolish	Liberal	Selfish
Benevolent	Frugal	Miserly	Sensible
Big-hearted	Generous	Modest	Spendthrift
Cautious	Grateful	Obsessive	Stingy
Charitable	Greedy	Openhanded	Thrifty
Cheap	Hesitant	Philanthropic	Wasteful
Comfortable	Hoarding	Poor	Wealthy
Compulsive	Ignorant	Possessive	Well informed
Confident	Impoverished	Prosperous	Wise
Conservative	Impulsive	Protective	Worried

- How do your values relate to your perspectives and beliefs about money?
- Are there people with whom you can comfortably talk about your money issues – your partner or spouse, your children, siblings, parents, friends, professionals?

Personal Money History

As a product of my generation, I still hear echoes of "don't worry your pretty little head about it" from the 1950s and "money's dirty" from I'm not sure where. This makes me afraid of money, of being dumb. And if I'm smart about money, will I be considered unfeminine?

I recall feeling humiliated when a solicitor told me how much I "should" give to her charitable organization. She knew nothing about my circumstances – at the time we were living on my teacher's salary and my husband was in graduate school. Unable to give, I felt ashamed and beat a hasty retreat to my shelter of choice: contempt for the solicitor and her organization.

Years later, after my financial situation had improved, I felt another kind of shame. I was riding the subway in New York when a pregnant homeless woman entered the car. I immediately looked away. As she walked through the car, begging unsuccessfully, she began a furious tirade that silenced us all. She said that it was okay if we didn't give her money, she just wanted someone to look her in the eyes and acknowledge her existence, because she was a human being too. She then strode, outraged, into the next car. I was stunned. For the first time I saw how my discomfort could lead to inhumane behavior. I vowed never again to avoid eye contact with a person less fortunate than I.

In my thirties – the height of my disdain – I fantasized about leaving civilization and going to live in the woods, where money would

Finance has to do with judgment and instinct and the ability to learn, three characteristics women have in abundance. What women do not have is comfort, confidence and trust in handling their money themselves or in handing its care over to someone else.

– Frances Lear

be unnecessary. I had just returned from serving in the Peace Corps, living amid people for whom lifelong poverty was a reality. Paradoxically, I now found myself riding in a golf cart at the country club that my husband and I had joined. Conflicted, I had to let go of my fantasy. Avoiding money would make no difference in a world of plenty where children go hungry. I let go of the country club as well, ashamed at participating in such expensive exclusivity.

I've joked about my acquisitive habits, my inability to resist clever marketing techniques, my tendency to impulse-buy. But I'm working seriously, and slowly, on simplifying my life. I fantasize about how wealthy I'll be when the world economy fails. With my collection of stunning stones and carefully picked seashells, I'll have lots to barter with.

For me, money has been an uncomfortable topic – and I'm not alone. As women, we know that family, society, and experience have shaped our perceptions about money. Nevertheless, when we examine our financial histories we are often surprised at the negative feelings that arise.

Don't waste. Whether it be time, resources, or money, waste is a sin.

– Sharon Strassfeld

REFLECTION AND WRITING   (45 to 60 minutes)

Get comfortable in your sacred writing space, then think of as many memories related to money as you can. Use the following questions to stimulate your reflection. Then, write about your experiences with money, letting your memory trail guide you. Because of the emotionality of this topic, consider writing your thoughts on one side of the paper and feelings on the other. You may need to set aside your writing and come back to it after a day or even two. Several short writing sessions can accomplish your goal just as well as one long session.

- What were your early experiences with money? Did you perceive a lack or an abundance of money in your family when you were growing up? Did you have an allowance? Were you paid to do certain chores? If you received money as a child, were you given guidelines about how to use it? Were you expected to share your money or give any of it to help others? Did you consider the money "yours"?

- Reflect on your family's explicit and implicit attitudes about money. How do you feel about this legacy? In what ways were your parents positive and negative role models for earning, saving, spending, and giving? In what ways do you handle money like your mother? Like your father?

- Have you inherited money? Are these funds separate from your everyday finances? How do you use the money you've inherited? Do you make charitable contributions with your inherited money?

- Consider your experiences with money as an adult – areas of comfort and discomfort, conflict and harmony, secrecy and openness. Do you generally believe that you are blessed with abundance, or do you feel the pinch of scarcity?

- How do you get money? If you have a partner, how does money affect your relationship? Do you make financial decisions alone, with a partner, or with others in your family?

- Are you comfortable spending money on yourself for your basic needs? For luxuries? For fun? What are your limits for spending on yourself? Are you generous or stingy with yourself?

- Do you spend money on others? Do you regularly buy gifts for those you love? Do you give money to others? How do you decide how much to spend or give?

- Have you ever given to charitable causes or to individuals less fortunate than you? Why or why not? Have you ever given to a homeless person? To someone begging? How do you feel about being asked for money? How do you decide how much, to whom, and when you will give? Do you make charitable contributions as a family? How do you decide on amounts and recipients?

If you are working in a legacy circle, you may want to restate the confidentiality rule — what is said within the circle doesn't leave the circle — before you decide whether to share part or all of your writing. Working with women you trust can help you hone your direction, refine your insight, deepen your compassion, and strengthen your power.

Anticipating My Financial Needs

Saving and investing for our future may be the only way to predict our future.
— Frances Lear

We are often told, in this day and age, that we must take care of ourselves if we expect to care for others. But society teaches women to give, give, give, and we've been well trained. We have a lot to learn about self-care. This, coupled with our taboos concerning money, makes it challenging to consider our financial needs for the future. But unless we plan for ourselves, we will not be adequately prepared to consider the financial aspects of the legacies we wish to leave.

REFLECTION AND WRITING
~ *Part 1*   *(45 to 60 minutes)*

No matter your age, marital status, or financial situation today, visualize yourself at a time in the future — five, ten, even twenty-five years from now. Imagine that you are on your own financially. Write about what you see, using the following prompts:

- What is your monetary situation? What kind of lifestyle do you have? How are you maintaining this lifestyle?
- What are your personal care needs and healthcare costs?
- What are you spending your money on? Do you have adequate funds to meet your basic needs? Do you have additional money for books, travel, restaurants, and other luxuries?
- Can you go where you want, do what you want, buy what you want?
- Has your budget shrunk or increased in the last decade?

Now, return to the present moment and write about your experience.

- What surprised you about your trip into the future?
- What can you do today to prepare for the future?
- How will you ensure that you'll have what you need as you age?
- Are there attitudes about money that you want to change? How can you make these changes?
- Do you need counsel, perhaps from a trusted friend, a professional, a financial advisor?

~ *Part 2*   *(no time limit)*

Write out a plan for your financial future, a blueprint for action. Since this is new territory for many women, share your ideas with someone you trust — a friend, family member, or the women in your legacy circle. It may help to have support as you begin your financial planning.

Handling the Inheritance

Unless we make specific arrangements, our money will automatically be distributed according to state probate laws after we die. For some women this may be acceptable, but most feel strongly about determining where their money will go.

Many women leave some money for loved ones, generally their children or grandchildren. The question of whether and how much to give, however, is complex. Your choices range from leaving the maximum possible inheritance, regardless of need, to no inheritance at all. You may want to consider how you want the money to be used — in a manner consistent with your values or at the recipients' discretion. You may need to find a creative way to communicate your preference.

Carol, a single woman and lifelong professional, decided to leave part of her estate to her three nieces and her nephew. Because she had

Take care of yourself and your family first. This is not an easy one for me. Creating the right priorities is something I've struggled with all my life, so I know how important it is.
— Sharon Strassfeld

strong feelings about making a difference in the community, she wanted to bequeath a spiritual message as well. Carol believed that her heirs would come to understand the importance of giving not through her words, but through their own experience. So, working with professionals to set up her estate, she stipulated that a percentage of the annual payout would go to the charitable cause of each recipient's choice. She then used her spiritual-ethical will, which is not a legal document, to explain her values and what she hoped to accomplish with her gift.

In this exercise you will explore options for distributing your financial legacy. You will explain to your loved ones how you arrived at your decisions and which values you hope to impart along with your money. This may be a difficult aspect of your legacy work. It requires creativity to use your money in a way that integrates your values with your desire to give. Further, it demands the courage to give voice to your decisions. This challenge is about your self-respect and integrity. Your intellect, your values, and your deepest spiritual beliefs will guide these important decisions.

My family believes in giving charity every time you do a business deal. That means whether you make or lose money, you must set aside money for charity.
– Sharon Strassfeld

REFLECTION AND WRITING
~ *Part 1* *(15 to 30 minutes)*

Many people, among them the very wealthy, plan to distribute most of their wealth to charitable causes rather than to their children. They cite numerous reasons: handing money to the children may do more harm than good; if the kids earn it themselves, they'll develop an appreciation for it; it's more important to contribute to healing the problems of society. When substantial amounts of money are involved, some parents express concern about their children's self-esteem if they don't need to work to support themselves. In these cases, many people decide on an upper limit for their children's inheritance – beyond that amount, they plan to contribute their money where it will do the most good.

Other parents feel a strong obligation to their children. They have supported and protected their children all their lives, and they see no reason to stop after their deaths. These people hope to give their heirs a leg up – providing a safety net, a down payment on a house, college tuition for a grandchild. They trust their children to use the money responsibly.

Take time to review your writings from chapters 5 through 8. With these perspectives firmly in mind, write your preliminary thoughts about giving – or not giving – to loved ones. Stay within the time limit, and write for as many days as needed until you have fully explored your ideas and feel ready to move forward.

~ *Part 2*   *(30 to 60 minutes)*

If you have decided not to leave a portion of your financial legacy to loved ones, skip this step and move on to part 3. Otherwise, use the allotted time to explore the following:

- How much money do you want to leave to your family: some, most, or all of your financial legacy? Be as clear and truthful as you can.
- Consider how you will distribute your money among your heirs. Is age a consideration? Do you have a child with special needs? Do you have one child who is more financially successful than the others? Consider how these differences influence your decisions about the inheritance. In this world of blended families, will you differentiate between your own children and your stepchildren?
- If you distribute the money equally, what are your reasons? If you divide the inheritance according to need or other considerations, what issues might this raise among your heirs?
- Would you consider sharing a portion of your financial legacy with people other than your children and grandchildren – nieces, nephews, parents, cousins, nonrelatives?
- What values do you want to pass on with your money? Will you want to influence the use of the money? Do you want to ensure that a portion of the inheritance is tithed annually to charitable causes?

- How would you feel if one or more of your heirs failed to handle their inheritance in a responsible way?
- Is this money an outright gift? Is it a reward for your loved ones' values and achievements? Why do you want your heirs to have this money?
- How do you want to distribute this money – in one payment, or parceled out over time? Will you designate trustees to oversee distribution? Will you set the money aside until the recipients reach a certain age? Will you distribute part or all of this money before your death?
- How might this inheritance complicate your loved ones' values or life challenges?

~ *Part 3*   *(30 to 60 minutes)*

Now that you've thoroughly explored your reasons for giving or not giving, write a letter explaining how you arrived at your decisions. If you are giving any portion of your financial legacy to loved ones, be sure to discuss the values you hope to impart with your gift. Then, set this letter aside with the other materials to be included in your spiritual-ethical will.

Leaving Money to Charitable Causes

And of all that You give me, I will set aside a tithe for You.

– Gen. 28:22

Tikkun olam, a concept from Jewish mystical tradition, means "repairing the world." How did the world become in need of repair? Tradition tells us that God tried to contain the holy light, the first creation, in vessels. But the light was so bright that the vessels burst and shattered. Discord and confusion spread as the light flew to every corner of the universe. So, God created us as partners, challenging us to find and collect the shards of light and repair the broken world.

Contributing to charitable causes is one of many ways to repair the world – something that Elena, a sculptor, tried to keep in mind when she unexpectedly received a large inheritance. First she decided

Charitable Causes

Animal welfare	Hunger
Arts and culture	International relief and development
Children and families	Media and freedom of expression
Civil rights	Peace and human rights
Death and dying	Religion and spirituality
Economic and social justice	Scientific research
Education	Seniors
Environment	Sports and recreation
Ethics	Veterans
Gay and lesbian rights	Violence against women and children
Health and medicine	Women's rights
Homelessness	

how much she would need for herself, then she determined how much she wanted to pass on to her children. But when she tried to contribute a percentage of her inheritance to a community fund, she found herself unable to sign the documents. She'd come up against an issue she'd struggled with all her life: fear of losing control. Finally she sought counsel with her spiritual advisor, who asked, "How will the world be better because you have lived?" With these words Elena was able to move forward, integrating her need for control with her strong commitment to do what she could to repair the world. She met with the community fund officer, and together they worked out a plan allowing her to direct the charity's use of her contributions. Taking a hands-on approach to make a difference in the world became a personally empowering – and spiritually satisfying – part of her legacy.

Giving is a spiritual act, one that feels natural to many women. We give our time, effort, and heart; we spend countless hours stamping envelopes, making telephone calls, feeding the homeless, and assisting families in crisis. We give so much, in fact, that the Independent Sector's report, "Giving and Volunteering in the United States," values volunteer services rendered in 2001 at $239 billion.

Our tendency to give of ourselves is only a hop, skip, and jump away from giving money, and it is no surprise that more and more women are finding ways to use their money to repair the world. We are beginning to shift our thinking, to empower ourselves, to realize that our financial contributions make an impact.

Giving to charitable causes is not just an opportunity for the rich; it's something anyone can do. As little as we may have, there are always those who have less. To quote a Minnesota schoolteacher, "My estate will never be large enough to be able to build libraries, but it may be large enough to buy some books for a library."

Why Give?

To establish immortality

To fulfill our life purpose

To leave an imprint on society

To make a significant difference

To do our part to heal the world

To feel like our life has made a difference

To fulfill a responsibility in our community

To perpetuate our philosophy or perspective

To give back in gratitude for our abundance

To deepen our spiritual life and commitment

To help our favorite charity accomplish its mission

To memorialize and honor our family or ethnic group

To connect with others who share our passions and interests

To experience the satisfaction of knowing we've done something worthwhile

Give of yourself…. No one has ever become poor from giving.
— Anne Frank

For many of us, charitable giving is of the utmost importance. If we don't make charitable bequests, we surrender our last chance to make a difference in the world. Worse, unless we have a legal will, some or all of our funds may go by default to the government. Then our money may be used to develop weapons of mass destruction or drill for oil in the wilderness, when we wanted it used to feed children, shelter abused women, protect endangered species, fund the arts, or support education.

REFLECTION AND WRITING   *(30 to 90 minutes)*

You are no doubt committed to any number of social or political causes. To determine where your money will do the most good, you will need to consider what, specifically, you want your financial legacy to accomplish. For example, if you feel passionate about supporting education, you might focus on literacy, tutoring, scholarships, adult learning, diversity programs, a lecture series, books for media centers, or programs to encourage young women in math and science.

Next, you'll need to seek out organizations that might be a good fit. The Internet offers a wealth of information, and most organizations provide Web sites displaying their mission statements and other details. Before making a donation, be sure to investigate an organization's credibility and fiscal responsibility, and find out exactly how your money will be used.

To get started in your research, you might contact GuideStar or the Better Business Bureau Wise Giving Alliance. Both organizations offer descriptions of various nonprofits, assistance in evaluating organizations, and credible reports on charities in the United States and abroad.

GuideStar
427 Scotland Street
Williamsburg, Virginia 23185
www.guidestar.org
757-229-4631

Better Business Bureau Wise Giving Alliance
4200 Wilson Boulevard, Suite 800
Arlington, Virginia 22203
www.give.org
703-276-0100

An old woman planting an olive tree was asked if she expected to benefit from its fruit or shade. She responded that she wasn't planting for herself, but for her children and grandchildren. "I found fully grown trees in the world. As my ancestors planted for me, so I plant for the generations to come."

– a retelling of a story from the Talmud

Once you determine how much you want to give and to whom, you will need professional assistance in drawing up a legal will to document your gifts. (See "Choosing a Professional" below.) But first, take sixty to ninety minutes to write about your reasons for giving. Do this for yourself, for your professional advisor, and, most important, for the recipients of your spiritual-ethical will. Your loved ones will value a clarification of your goals and decisions. They will appreciate knowing how you integrated your financial legacy with your love for them and your passion to repair the world.

Begin by listing the reasons for your decisions. Then, use the letter-writing technique to expand on these reasons. Include examples, descriptions, and anecdotes to express yourself fully. Address your letter to those who will inherit your financial legacy. When you are finished, file this letter with your other materials for your spiritual-ethical will.

Choosing a Professional

A sphere is made up of not one, but an infinite number of circles; women have diverse gifts, and to say that women's sphere is the family circle is a mathematical absurdity.

– Maria Mitchell

To legitimize your financial gifts, or to gather input before making decisions, you will need the help of a professional advisor. Remember, your spiritual-ethical will does not take the place of a legal document. In order to ensure the distribution of your financial legacy according to your plan, you must provide for it legally. For many women, this means venturing into what seems an alien, hostile world. Armed with passionate purpose, thoughtful planning, and what you have written, however, you can walk confidently into the office of an estate planner, an attorney, maybe even an accountant.

To locate an advisor, ask friends, family, and the women in your legacy circle for referrals. Leave a Legacy (www.leavealegacy.org), The Legacy Center (www.thelegacycenter.net), and the Society of Financial Service Professionals (www.financialpro.org) can also direct you to attorneys, trust officers, and other advisors in your area. Be sure to interview several advisors. Remember, you are in a powerful position as a potential customer. Give yourself permission to hire someone else if your first choice doesn't work out. Be especially wary of professionals who maintain an uncomfortable distance by using technical or exclusive language, who have their own agenda or interests, who trivialize your concerns, or whose ethics you question. The person you choose should listen and communicate well, treat you with respect, and fully support your legacy plan.

Once you begin working with a professional advisor, be honest about who you are and what you're trying to do. If you don't understand something, ask for clarification. Don't sell yourself short: there are no stupid questions, and every question deserves a respectful answer. If you feel nervous about the initial meeting, you might ask a trusted friend to accompany you.

As you work with your advisor, you may decide to keep a journal of your thoughts about this challenging subject, perhaps including it in your spiritual-ethical will. What a wonderful gift for your daughters and granddaughters, who, in a different time, will consider such writing historical, just as we view the writings by women who fought for the vote more than eighty years ago.

If you own something you don't need, give it away to someone who can use it. Many people are afraid to do this, since they think there may come a time when they need the thing they've given away. Believe me, it's better to give it away.
– Sharon Strassfeld

A Vietnamese Folktale

A woman visiting Hell was amazed to find the inhabitants sitting across from each other at beautifully arranged tables with ivory chopsticks, delicate tableware, and bountiful food. Yet no one was eating, and all were wailing. When she looked closely, she saw that the chopsticks were three feet long, and the people could not bring the food to their mouths.

The visitor then went to Heaven, where she found a nearly identical scene: beautifully arranged tables with ivory chopsticks, delicate tableware, and bountiful food. Here, too, the chopsticks were three feet long, yet no one was wailing – because each person was serving the person across from her.

CHAPTER TEN

On Death and Dying

Several years ago I presented my five-year-old granddaughter, Sophie, with a blank book, a granddaughter-grandmother journal. This journal, I explained, was just for us. She wouldn't have to share it with any of the other grandchildren. Each time we were together we would write or draw in our special journal, then we'd put it away in a secret place in my writing room. Because Sophie wasn't writing yet, I would be the scribe and she could decide what we would write about. When she was a little older, we would share responsibility for the writing.

Sophie's eyes sparkled as we looked excitedly at all the blank pages. She picked out a pink marker, printed her name on the first page, and beautified it with a heart or two. Witnessing the birth of a natural journal writer, I imagined the wonderful events, thoughts, and feelings that would fill this record of our relationship. As Sophie looked up at me with her innocent, dark eyes, she happily exclaimed, "Oh, I get it, Granny! Then when you're dead I'll know everything that we did together."

She got it! My eyes filled with tears, my heart with the bittersweet reality of love and death – the truth she so easily understood and accepted. One day she would have our special journal, and I wouldn't be here to enjoy her anymore.

Documenting a legacy addresses a deep need to be remembered, a need we all share. It implies an awareness of mortality, an acknowledgment that one day we will no longer be alive. This is a difficult certainty to confront. Yet throughout history, women have cared for the dying, comforted mourners, and laid out the dead. Our intimacy with birth and death makes us part of a worldwide community of women who greet these wonders with love and awe. Above all, it teaches us that death, like life, is precious and sacred.

Legacy writing is an opportunity to honor our death as well as our life, clearly communicating how we want to be remembered. We can express idiosyncratic wishes related to our death, funeral, and burial, and we can ask our families to honor these wishes. In Genesis, where the ethical will originated, Jacob first blessed his sons and then instructed them to return his bones to his ancestors' burial place:

"I am about to be gathered to my kin. Bury me with my fathers in the cave which is in the field of Ephron the Hittite, the cave which is in the field of Machpelah, facing Mamre, in the land of Canaan, the field that Abraham bought from Ephron the Hittite for a burial site – there Abraham and his wife Sarah were buried; there Isaac and his wife Rebekah were buried; and there I buried Leah – the field and the cave in it, bought from the Hittites." When Jacob finished his instructions to his sons, he drew his feet into the bed and, breathing his last, he was gathered to his people. (Gen. 49:29–33)

Because none of us know when and under what circumstances our end will come, it's imperative that we document our preferences and instructions while we are of sound mind. In the following pages we

The most remarkable thing about death is its insistence on harvesting life's meaning, even in those not prone to introspection.
– Joan Borysenko

I still grieve for the words unsaid. Something terrible happens when we stop the mouths of the dying before they are dead. A silence grows up between us, profounder than the grave. If we force the dying to go speechless, the stone dropped into the well will fall forever before the answering splash is heard.
– Faye Moskowitz

The Death of Jacob
Genesis 49

As Jacob lay dying
he had strength to bless his sons
and time to speak his prophecies.

But in our time
death is a hungry hunter
pursuing us on the highway,
overtaking us in the fastest planes;

Dying, there may be for us no long farewells,
no blessings, and no prophecies.

Living, then, we must bless our children,
placing our hands upon them
and turning their faces toward God;
living, we must struggle for a better day.

To foretell the future
may be a patriarch's privilege,
but to take the future in our hands is urgent
and to make it good shall be our human glory.

Oh God of Jacob, while yet we live,
help us to guide our children in love and wisdom,
help us now to build a world of peace.

– from *Harvest,* by Ruth F. Brin

will examine how we want to be remembered, then we'll organize our instructions for our survivors. For those who are overwhelmed at the thought of putting their affairs in order, completing this chapter will bring a welcome sense of relief.

Naturally, the decisions you make today may change over time. As you update these sections of your spiritual-ethical will, you might keep a record of your writings to document your personal growth.

Forgetfulness leads to exile, while memory leads to redemption.
– Baal Shem Tov

What I'll Miss When I'm Gone

It is true that our lives will betray us in the end but life knows where it is going.
– Linda Hogan

A dramatic way to clarify how we want to be remembered by others is to consider what we've valued most about life on earth. This perspective awakens our gratitude to the abundant blessings in our lives, making the most mundane details seem sacred. Consider what you have taken for granted. What will you miss?

REFLECTION AND WRITING

Rather than to do this exercise all at once, you might prefer to do it for short periods of time over several days. When you are finished, consider including this writing as part of your legacy – just as it is, in your own handwriting and from your heart. While other parts of your spiritual-ethical will are meant to be edited and revised (see chapter 12), let this writing stand spontaneous and uncensored. Let the future see your passion for life.

~ *Part 1*   *(10 to 20 minutes)*

Reflect on what you love most in your life. At the top of the page write "What I Will Miss When I Die." Begin each sentence with "I'll miss . . ." and write as much as you can in the time allotted. For example, "I'll miss feeling the dew on the grass when I go barefoot to pick fresh tomatoes from my garden."

I'll miss my children, husband, family, my dog.

I will miss my favorite time of year, when blossoms burst forth and multitudes of color splash through my garden in many shapes, forms, and textures.

I will miss the blue of the sky, as well as the clouds that blow with the wind and cover the large, yellow ball of light.

I will miss the darkness and quiet that bring peace, reflection, and solitude to my otherwise hectic day.

I will miss the beauty of my relationships and the women who have known and supported me for most of my adult life.

I will miss the smell and taste of my mother's bread as the butter and cinnamon melt, making my mouth water and my stomach growl.

I will miss the feel of the black dirt as I dig and plant and water and feel the energy of the sun, knowing that the earth holds a miracle to produce such beauty as to satisfy all my senses.

I will miss the sunlight and the sense that when I open my eyes in the morning to a new day, it has the potential to create miracles and possibilities and blessings, because I am alive and free and able to love and return to the earth the blessings it has given me.

– Pamela R. Borgmann

Be specific. Write about things that only you know of, that you care deeply about, that will die with you if you don't record them. Slow down; notice and remember those details you don't ordinarily take time to appreciate. Let yourself feel how much you will miss these things when your life is over. Focus on smelling, touching, hearing, seeing, tasting: "I'll miss the sound of a canoe paddle dipped into a calm lake." Consider the relational, social, familial, or communal: "I'll miss reading for the blind."

When you have completed the exercise, set the list aside for a day. Then, read your list aloud. What you read may surprise and touch you, stimulating even more thoughts to add to your list. If you are working in a legacy circle, have each woman read one item, going around and around until everyone has shared all the items on her list. If you hear something that you want to add to your own list, do so. At the end of this exercise, give yourself a few minutes to record your response to this writing.

~ *Part 2* *(15 minutes)*

Choose one idea from your list and write about it for the allotted time. Repeat this exercise as many days as you wish, perhaps expanding on your other values.

How Will I Be Remembered

You don't get to choose how you're going to die. Or when. You can only decide how you're going to live. Now.
– Joan Baez

It's only normal to want to be remembered. By living on in other people's memories, we ensure our immortality. As Barbara, a recovering breast cancer patient, told her legacy circle, "I intend to survive this disease. Nevertheless, having permission to write about the end of my life has given me a sense of peace." She used her writing to confront her fears about dying, to clarify the value of her life, and to show her family how she wanted to be remembered after she died.

In this exercise you will write about your life from the perspective of your death. But first, imagine that you could take a snapshot of your life at this very moment. What would you see? How would others remember you? More important, how would you hope to be remembered?

We have to make myths of our lives. It is the only way to live without despair.

– May Sarton

REFLECTION AND WRITING

You will complete this writing over the course of several days. Write for no longer than the time allotted each day. Record your process afterward, reflecting on your thoughts and feelings.

~ *Part 1* *(15 minutes)*

Imagining that you have died, write about yourself in the third person. Complete the following sentence as many times as you can: "At the time of her death, she was. . . ." Was what?

For example, "At the time of her death, she was groping toward a new beginning. At the time of her death, she was in love with her life. At the time of her death, she was running scared. At the time of her death, she'd finally stopped trying to meet the expectations of others."

~ *Part 2* *(15 minutes)*

Expand on one of your sentences from part 1, considering the context of your statement. Add an explanation for clarification. Is this how you think you will be remembered? Is it how you want to be remembered? If not, how can you change your life today so that you will be remembered differently? Write about one entry a day for as many days as you wish.

~ *Part 3* *(30 minutes)*

Write a statement that could be read at your memorial, used in your obituary, or inscribed on your headstone. You might want to include this writing

Dear Asher,

This letter is about the feeling of fullness. It is an extremely important concept to me and one that I think is essential for a good life. It is important because, in my life, I have been a person who has often felt empty. And because of my personal experience with the feeling of emptiness, I have come to understand that the feeling of fullness is one of the most blessed, most unacknowledged, and most underrated feelings I know. I do not mean happiness, nor do I mean contentment, nor do I mean peacefulness. I mean, very simply, that you feel there is enough inside you, that you feel internally rich and varied. That there are no big empty spaces, no holes that gnaw at the fabric of your being. I am also talking about the size human being you experience yourself to be: large or small; generous and expansive, or tight and pinched and hoarding.

Fullness has many meanings. It may mean that you have enough of an inner sense of self to feel that the space within you can be filled up. It may mean your ability to take experiences and turn them into gratifications. There is another meaning of the word fullness that I wish for you and this has to do with the enlargement of your own feeling and perception. I believe that a feeling of fullness arises from the mind's ability to see, notice, and make discriminations between and within categories of things, persons, and events. To put this assumption very simply: the more you can see, the richer your life will be, the more diverse your experience, and therefore, the fuller you can be.

The finer the discriminations one can make, the more precise the perceptions, the more vivid the details, the tinier each piece of information is, the fuller and richer will be the picture you have. Each detail is a particular slice of information, each is to be observed and to be savored. The smaller your discriminations, the richer is your picture of the world and, in turn, the richer your internal life. Your internal landscape may be filled with more units of perception and concentration than perhaps you will know what to do with. Let it be. May you be blessed with an enlarged capacity to discern.

Imagine the depth and breadth of your ability to become more human as you begin to recognize and identify the different types of human experience. Your ability to grow, change, and develop will depend on how much you can discriminate and then empathize with different kinds of human experience.

Let us take, for example, different types of human pain. There is grief. There is sorrow. There is loss. There is disappointment. The more you can tell the difference between each one of these experiences, and the more you can understand each one in its particularity, the more human and alive you can become. The world will be a more complex place and it is within complexity that you can locate richness and diversity of experience.

And, finally, there can be no richness and sense of fullness without others. We take others within our selves, into our souls, to inhabit us and live with us for a while, sometimes even a lifetime. May these occupants of your soul, these introjects, these ghosts, these ancestors, these tenants be benevolent and kind, generous and loving. May you live in common cause with them, not in struggle and conflict. May they illuminate you from inside, letting light shine through you. May you have the generosity of spirit to let them sing through you. May you be expansive enough to surrender part of yourself, to allow yourself to be a vessel for these ancient voices, these ancient truths, these cries filled with mystery and nobility that may possess you in the most unexpected moments.

I wish for you that most of your emptinesses are fillable. I wish for you that you can live with some degree of emptiness, allowing it its own space, allowing it to be the spacious and merciful quiet that it can be. May you not rush to fill it with noise and cheap affections.

As paradoxical as it all sounds, may you be the empty vessel of active agency so that you can have a full and rich life. There is nothing better. Take this from me on faith. I know. I have it and I grieve to lose it.

Love, Aunt Barbara, January 4, 1988

— from *Cancer in Two Voices,*
by Sandra Butler and Barbara Rosenblum

as part of your spiritual-ethical will, knowing that you can change or update it at any time. If you want your survivors to use this writing to memorialize you after you die, you'll have a chance to communicate this preference at the end of the chapter.

Death Rituals

Several years ago a friend of mine died after a long fight with pancreatic cancer. She had preplanned her funeral, with the guidance of her female rabbi, and invited her closest friends to be her pallbearers. At the conclusion of the memorial service, the rabbi announced that the deceased had requested a special song to be played as she was taken from the sanctuary. The pallbearers – all women – rose and took their places, the sound system came on, and Frank Sinatra sang "I Did It My Way." We all wept at the loss of her; the song only made our tears flow faster. She had done her life and her death "her way." Now, remembering her humor, her strength of will, and her uniqueness, we had to face that she was gone.

Death rituals, whether personalized or rooted in tradition, bring comfort and support to mourners while honoring the sacred life of the deceased. They offer a sense of timelessness, of community, of spiritual connection. In Jewish tradition, for example, family and friends may each place a shovelful of earth onto a loved one's casket before leaving the cemetery. The shovel is held scoop-side down, symbolizing the mourners' reluctance to say goodbye. This ritual marks a profound shift in the survivors' relationship with the deceased. In the comforting presence of community they can begin to face the reality of death, to mourn, and to remember.

In this exercise you'll choose rituals for your own funeral or memorial. Later, you can document your wishes in your spiritual-ethical will.

It is only past the meridian of fifty that one can believe that the universal sentence of death applies to oneself.
– May Sarton

Tombstones mark time with eternity.
– Natalie Goldberg

REFLECTION AND WRITING

~ *Part 1*   *(45 to 60 minutes)*

Mourning rituals are often legacies handed down from generation to generation through families and faith communities. What does your family or community traditionally do when a loved one dies? Describe any of the following:

- Does your family participate in a religious ceremony? If so, does it include particular music or readings? Are there other details – bells, incense, prayers, songs, drumming, blessings, candles, flowers? Where does the ceremony take place?
- Does your family hold a wake or viewing? If so, where?
- Are special items placed in the casket with the deceased? How is the body dressed?
- Does your family prefer burial or cremation? Describe the burial rights or the scattering of the ashes.
- Are mourners invited to share a meal in honor of the deceased? Are special foods served?
- Does your family observe particular mourning rituals – lighting candles, decorating the grave with flowers, stopping clocks, covering mirrors, cutting off hair, wearing certain symbols or colors, or placing a stone on the grave to mark each visit? How do these rituals help you remember the deceased?
- How does your family mark the anniversary of a death?

~ *Part 2*   *(30 to 60 minutes)*

Many women embrace traditional family or ethnic rituals, imbuing them with personal meaning. Others create their own death rituals, hoping to distance themselves from traditions that no longer provide solace or support.

Describe the rituals that are meaningful to you, and express your reasons for wanting to be remembered in these ways. Write about rituals that you definitely want or don't want your loved ones to use when celebrating your life or memorializing your death.

Post Humus

Scatter my ashes in my garden
so I can be near my loves.
Say a few honest words,
sing a gentle song,
join hands in a circle of flesh.
Please tell some stories
about me making you laugh.
I love to make you laugh.

When I've had time to settle
and green gathers into buds,
remember I love blossoms
bursting in spring.
As the season ripens
remember my persistent passion.

And if you come in my garden
on an August afternoon,
pluck a bright red globe,
let juice run down your chin
and the seeds stick to your cheek.

When I'm dead I want folks to smile
and say, "That Patti, she sure is
some tomato!"

                                        – Patti Tana

Take as much time as you need to determine which rituals you'd like to have at your own funeral or memorial. You might enlist friends to help research old and new ideas. Sharing in your legacy circle may yield further ideas and expand your options. Resources that may aid your research include *A Woman's Journey to God,* by Joan Borysenko; *Lifecycles,* edited by Debra Orenstein; and *Flames to Heaven,* by Debbie Perlman.

Remember that this is your personal – and preliminary – exploration. You are free to change your mind, and you probably will as you continue to consider rituals that resonate with how you want to be remembered. You may want to return to this topic from time to time, reflecting on the complexity and significance of finding rituals consonant with who you are. In the next exercise you'll learn how to effectively communicate your preferences to your survivors.

Easing the Way for Our Loved Ones

More than anything, we want to deliver our loved ones from suffering and sadness – an impossible goal that is not always in their best interests. Though your loved ones will be bereaved when you die, they have the right, the need, and the responsibility to mourn their loss. You can't take their grief away, nor should you try.

Your loved ones will need to mourn in order to heal. They will need to experience their feelings and integrate a new reality: living in the world without you. Mourning is not about forgetting, for we all know that relationships continue beyond the grave. Rather, it is the process of reconstructing a relationship with the deceased in a manner that allows for a continuing but changing bond.

Though grief is both essential and inevitable, you can ease your loved ones' pain by communicating your healthcare and memorial wishes in advance. In so doing, you will spare survivors the agony of

Making up a will is difficult for some people. There's a superstitious belief that as long as the will has not been done, they can't die.

– Ram Dass

wondering whether they made the right decisions on your behalf. Moreover, you will give them an opportunity to honor you in death by respecting your wishes.

REFLECTION AND WRITING

In this exercise you will document your healthcare preferences in the event of a serious illness or accident, and you will share some thoughts on how you want your life to be memorialized. Finally, you will gather all your wishes and instructions in one location for loved ones to read after you die.

~ *Part 1*   *(30 minutes)*

If you have ever been with a dying loved one who received treatments contrary to her values or preferences, you know how important it is to complete an advance directive. An advance directive is a signed, dated, and witnessed document that allows you to state your wishes regarding the use of life-prolonging medical treatment. Advance directives are sometimes called healthcare directives, durable powers of attorney for healthcare, or living wills. While the laws governing advance directives vary from state to state, your directive will likely document the following:

- The person you appoint to make healthcare decisions on your behalf, should you become unable to communicate your preferences
- What kind of medical treatment you want or don't want at the end of life
- Your concerns and preferences related to comfort and pain
- How you want to be cared for by loved ones (your wishes related to touch, massage, prayer, music, and other simple comfort measures)
- Thoughts and values to help guide decision-makers in your medical care

To prepare an advance directive, you will need the appropriate paperwork for your state. Contact any of the following to obtain the necessary materials:

- Your state board on aging, listed in your local phone book, can supply advance directive materials and instructions.

- Aging with Dignity offers "Five Wishes," an advance directive with a simple fill-in-the-blank format. Legal in most states, this inexpensive document is available at www.agingwithdignity.org. You may also call 1-888-5-WISHES, or mail your request to Aging with Dignity, P.O. Box 1661, Tallahassee, Florida 32302.
- The Community Alliance for Compassionate Care at the End of Life is another helpful resource. To request materials, call 417-865-4501, go to www.missouriendoflife.org, or write to Community Alliance, P.O. Box 5067, Springfield, Missouri 65801.

After you have gathered the necessary materials, take as many days as you need to absorb the content and resolve the complex issues raised. When you are ready, write a practice draft of your advance directive, following the instructions on the form. Set your writing aside for a day or two, then read it and edit it. Be gentle with yourself. If you feel too anxious to continue, stop and come back to the task tomorrow. Write for no more than thirty minutes a day. Continue this process until your words accurately express your decisions and preferences. Then, simply copy your words onto the actual form, finalizing your advance directive.

Once you have completed your directive, you must sign your document and have it witnessed. Give a copy of the directive to family members, your doctor, and other appropriate professionals. Each person should also receive a list of recipients. (Note that the "Five Wishes" packet includes specific directions for legalizing and filing your directive.)

Finally, it's a good idea to have a conversation with family and close friends so they know what you will want at the end of life. Clear communication will increase your chances of being treated as you prefer.

Of course, your treatment preferences may change over time, or you may need to select a new healthcare representative one day. In either case you must fill out a new directive. Be sure that each person who received your old directive is given a copy of the new one. You may update your advance directive as often as you wish.

To My Daughters
Exhortation to Prohibit Mourning on Cessation of the Motion of My Blood

Think of it this way
Now I'm exempt from all those arrows
Fate releases as she pleases,
Free from slings of nature and man.
As William phrases in his sonnet,
"Give not a windy night a rainy morrow"
  With massive sorrow.

Restrain liquidity, deplore excess
Rein in, in a mixed metaphor
The plunging pity of your tears.
One can't be witty
to a shroud.
   But don't be loud.

Death's invariably democratic, precise, concise
A constant in finality
I guarantee.
Our common equalizing – all of us at last.
So keep your saline squeezings hoarded
For Cassandrian crises.
You'll need them.

Secrete secret kinetic grief and lamentation
For future calamities.
I decree there'll be disasters
More astronomical than me.

I decline in all declensions
Mercy meted out in teaspoons.
Let's remember how it was
Make not minuscule our love.
Nor shrink expanded minds and hearts
Like laundered woe.
Don't dwarf emotions as I go
Now my December's here.
My autumn iced before the snow.

— Ella Berniece Bixler

~ *Part 2* *(45 minutes)*

Consider each item on the following list and commit your preferences to writing. You may wish to attach your writings from previous exercises as well. Don't let yourself become overwhelmed; take as many days as you need to research and contemplate these topics, but be sure to limit yourself to forty-five minutes a day. When you have finished, you will incorporate your information into part 3 of this exercise.

In the event of your death:
- Decisions about donating organs or tissue
- If you decide to donate your body for research, provide the name and contact information for the medical school or research laboratory

For your funeral[*] or memorial service:
- Preferred location: religious sanctuary, funeral home, graveside
- Preferred readings, songs, and other rituals
- Preferred charities for memorial donations

Burial or cremation:
- Location for burial: preferred cemetery; prepaid or family plot
- Words that you want on your tombstone
- Cremation: instructions for keeping or scattering your remains; request for a planting or other marker

~ *Part 3* *(no time limit)*

In this section, you will gather all relevant materials – important contacts, personal data, your legal will, your advance directive, a list of bequests, memorial instructions – and organize them for your survivors. When you complete your spiritual-ethical will, you will want to include this data with your other

[*]Note that *Consumer Reports* strongly advises against prepaying funerals (May 2001).

documents. If you decide not to share this information now, let your survivors know where they can find it later.

Take your time and be as thorough as you can. It may take several days to gather and organize this information. Begin with a master list, which can serve as a table of contents later on. You might include:

- Names and contact information for family, friends, and official advisors (clergy, physicians, attorneys, accountants, and estate or financial planners).
- Important documents and data, including your social security number, safe-deposit box key (note the location), computer codes and files, insurance policies, bank and credit card accounts, investment information, recent income tax returns, even frequent flyer miles and account numbers.
- A copy of your legal will.
- A copy of your advance directive.
- Special instructions for organ, tissue, and body donation.
- Preferences for your funeral, burial, cremation, or memorial, including words by which you would like to be remembered: perhaps an obituary, a eulogy, or a letter to be read at your memorial.
- A list of valuables you would like to bequeath, along with recipients' names and contact information. Attach your writings about the valued objects. (See page 146.)
- An explanation of your financial gifts to your heirs. (See page 170.)
- An explanation of your charitable donations. (See page 176.)

~

Congratulations. Having completed the work in this chapter, you've not only gained peace of mind, but taken an important step in organizing your spiritual-ethical will. Before finalizing this legacy document, you will want to consider one more aspect of your life: alternative legacies.

Loss is a magical preservative.

— Eva Hoffman

CHAPTER ELEVEN

$\mathcal{A}$lternative Legacies

We express our love for the future not just in our writing, but in our doing. Where up until now we've honored our individual voices with the written word, here we expand our understanding of legacy to accommodate our talents and good works. Whether we write poems, plant trees, crochet blankets for newborns, or document an elder's life story, each generous act leaves a powerful legacy to family and community.

Planting a Legacy

Healing our world happens one loving act at a time. Some acts may seem small, but each time we "think globally, act locally" we make a courageous contribution to the earth and all its life. Take Pamela R. Borgmann, for example. Pamela transformed a portion of her family farm into a tree memorial, where mourners gather to plant trees in remembrance of loved ones. What began as a family ritual to commemorate two lost brothers became a community tradition. Today, 350 people come from all over the country to visit this seven-acre site near Sauk Centre, Minnesota. Together they plant or visit their trees, shrubs, or perennials, share their grief, and remember their loved ones. "Mid-June in Minnesota is wildly gorgeous with color as flowers and green transform the frozen prairie," writes Pamela. "People gather at the Tree Memorial, greeting each other after the long, cold winter. They eat in community, plant and tend the gardens and arbors, tell stories of family members in the open air, and sing 'Amazing Grace' together. This tradition was conceived to honor the lives of our two brothers, and the first gathering included family and friends. Fifteen years and more than a thousand plantings later, our community legacy continues to blossom, a riot of colorful flowers among sacred trees that reach toward the sun above the flat prairie land. May this legacy of love continue to grow as the years pass."

Pamela has gathered written vignettes from the mourners to publish in a booklet titled *As We Remember: A Walking Guide through the Memorial.* By celebrating the legacies of both the living and the dead, this booklet will offer special gifts to those who visit the memorial in the future. In this excerpt, Robin and Amber Anderson write about planting a tree to honor Duane Hugh Anderson:

"We planted a weeping willow tree in memory of my husband and Amber's dad. He died at the age of fifty-nine on Veteran's Day, November 11, 1999. He was a hard worker in the sheet metal industry. We have wonderful memories of his music and his cooking. Amber inherited his talent for music, and he taught me a lot about cooking with his secret ingredients. He loved to make us happy by coming home with little gifts or treats for no special reason but to say I love you. Many years ago, after he was diagnosed with diabetes and heart disease, he taught me how to do all the

Bread feeds the body indeed, but flowers feed also the soul.
– *Qur'an*

Everybody needs beauty as well as bread, places to play in and pray in, where Nature may heal and cheer and give strength to body and soul alike.
– *John Muir*

'manly' jobs like lawn mowing, weed wacking, and snow blowing. I was being prepared for a time such as this. He was proud of us both. We were 'his girls.' "

If you decide to plant a tree, whether to honor a deceased loved one or leave a legacy for descendants, you might create a blessing ceremony so the sapling will carry the energy of your love. In *Sacred Legacies,* healer Denise Linn brings her Cherokee heritage to such work, noting that planting a generational tree is a sacred gift "that goes on giving long after you are gone." To mark the significance of a tree planting, she offers this blessing: "I dedicate this tree to [my] descendants and to the future generations that follow. May you help contribute to a future that is filled with trees and flowers and joy for all living beings. May the Creator who dwells in all things fill you with love and light and peace. May you provide shade, beauty, and healing for all who come in contact with you." If tree planting is a part of your legacy, be sure to document this in your spiritual-ethical will. You might include a written copy of the blessing you create, photographs of the sapling, progressive photographs of the tree's annual or biannual growth, and a recording of the planting ritual.

While perennial gardens, trees, bushes, and flowers offer powerful living legacies to the future, seeds hold an equally potent symbolism. Seeds signify fertility, seasonal growth, new beginnings, the potential for fulfillment. Around the globe, women, in particular, have had a strong association with seeds. Immigrant women smuggled seeds into the New World by sewing them into the hems of their skirts. Some Christian women wear mustard seed charms to remind them of the power of faith in their daily lives. A Greek bride, rather than throw her bouquet, may toss a pomegranate, a symbol of fertility due to its many seeds. And in China, the groom's family may present a new bride with a cup of tea containing lotus seeds, representing their hope for healthy grandchildren.

May we be filled with as many good deeds as the pomegranate is filled with seeds.

– Jewish liturgical blessing

Women's relationship with seeds and farming dates back to the beginning of recorded history. The early Greeks associated agriculture with the feminine principles of fertility and nurturance. In fact, many experts believe that women invented agriculture. Even in North America, native women were the first farmers, domesticating the wild plants found in the early hunting and gathering era.

"Historians have written a great deal about field agriculture in early America," notes Pulitzer Prize winning biographer Laurel Thatcher Ulrich, "but not enough about the intricate horticulture that belonged to women, the intense labor of cultivation and preservation that allowed one season to stretch almost to another." In *A Midwife's Tale: The Life of Martha Ballard, Based on Her Diary, 1785–1812,* Ulrich highlights an 1809 diary entry in which Ballard wrote about selling her seeds to Mrs. Emery and two of William Stone's children. Though she didn't philosophize about seeds living from generation to generation or suggest that the seeds she cultivated were part of her legacy, she proudly recorded that they "had garden seeds of me."

In recent years, many women have dedicated themselves to preserving heirloom seeds, ensuring the survival of healthy food sources and protecting endangered varieties. Judyth McLeod, author of *Heritage Gardening,* describes the importance of not only growing heirloom vegetables, but also sharing and saving the seeds to help protect plant diversity. "This is something real and concrete you can do for the world, something that can make a difference," says McLeod. "And, the traditional and heirloom fruits and vegetables you grow will return your kindness with the intense flavors of childhood memories and a willingness to grow as if they remember their traditional harmony and partnership with humanity."

REFLECTION AND WRITING

Many women report that their most spiritual moments have taken place in nature, yet too many of us are deprived of greenery and fresh air, living in an urban and homogenized world of paved patios, climate control, synthetic trees, and silk flowers. It's important to remember that every woman can reclaim a loving connection with the earth, no matter where she lives. Our legacy of love is expressed in every seed, flower, vegetable, and tree we plant. It is present when we conserve resources, recycle, share, hand things down, and hand things back. So whether you have acres of farmland, a small yard in the suburbs, an urban community garden, a single tomato plant on your apartment balcony, a lone houseplant on your windowsill, or a sapling on the fire escape (remember *A Tree Grows in Brooklyn*?), you are perpetuating a legacy for the earth and for the future.

~ *Part 1*   *(30 to 60 minutes)*

Consider all that you have planted and hope to plant, contemplating how these gifts are a component of your legacy. For example:

- Write about your favorite tree, plant, and flower. Help your descendants understand what they mean to you.
- What has gardening meant to you? Explore the practical, aesthetic, and healing components of gardening.
- If you have seeds, plants, or trees that you want to pass on, write the stories and significance of these gifts. Be sure to name the recipients in your spiritual-ethical will.

~ *Part 2*   *(30 to 60 minutes)*

List those things you love most in nature: oceans, lakes, mountains, prairies, woods; your favorite season; your fondness for animals. Reflect on the unique ways that you express your love for the earth. Share your passion for nature, documenting your love with a descriptive memory or story. Consider including this in your spiritual-ethical will.

We join with the earth and with each other
To bring new life to the land
To restore the waters
To refresh the air.

We join with the earth and with each other
To renew the forests
To care for the plants
To protect the creatures.

We join with the earth and with each other
To celebrate the seas
To rejoice in the sunlight
To sing the song of the stars.

We join with the earth and with each other
To recreate the human community
To promote justice and peace
To remember our children.

We join with the earth and with each other.
We join together as many and diverse expressions of one loving mystery:
     for the healing of the earth and the renewal of all life.

        – United Nations Environmental Sabbath Prayer

Documenting the Legacies of Others

Legacy writing in service to others is a moving gift of love and community-building. Across the nation, women are documenting the lives of aging relatives, sick or dying friends, residents at senior living facilities, and others who are unable to write for themselves. In *Bird by Bird,* Anne Lamott suggests that this gift to others can also be deeply healing for the writer – it has a very different value than writing for publication, fame, or money. "[There is] something to be said for painting portraits of the people we have loved, for trying to express those moments that seem so inexpressibly beautiful, the ones that change us and deepen us."

When Lamott's father was dying of cancer, she wrote about how she and her brothers were dealing with his illness and the idea of his dying, then read it to him in the months before his death – a gift of love. Fifteen years later, Lamott wrote about her best friend, Pammy, who was dying of cancer. "Pammy knew there was something that was going to exist on paper after she was gone, something that was going to be, in a certain way, part of her immortality."

Kathi Snead offered a similar gift to a dying friend, helping her to complete a spiritual-ethical will. Looking back on the experience, she writes, "My friend, Mary Lewis, died on May 20, 2002. She was forty-two years old and the mother of three children. Just three months earlier we had learned that Mary's breast cancer had returned and metastasized to other areas of her body. Mary was an employment counselor, a life coach, and a writer. She had often encouraged me to follow my dream of leading legacy and life story workshops.

"Before Mary died, I had come to realize the importance of documenting personal thoughts, feelings, values, and beliefs for one's children and grandchildren. I had been blessed with the joy of becoming a grandmother. Mary would never get that chance. She didn't even

Stories are for people what water is for plants.
– Linda Hogan

What did they do, our grandmothers, as they sat spinning all the day? Are we not ourselves the web they wove?
– Anonymous

have the chance to finish being a mom to the children she loved so dearly. I never imagined that the first person whom I would help write a spiritual-ethical will would be my dear friend.

"We started, writing fast and furiously, not knowing how much time we had. We wrote about her likes and dislikes, her beliefs and philosophy on life, her faith in God. In a letter that I gave to her children on the day she died, she recorded her favorite Bible verse, described what was special and unique about each child, and expressed her total and unconditional love.

"Writing with Mary was an incredible experience. There is no greater gift than helping a loved one express her feelings, her beliefs, her words. There is no greater gift we can give ourselves than the understanding and healing that comes with this type of writing. Just as an employment resumé provides a snapshot of one's work history and skills, a spiritual-ethical will gives your loved ones and family a picture of your soul, a portrait of who you really are."

Another way to bring healing to the world is to work with women in prisons or shelters. When I facilitated a legacy circle for a group of women serving life sentences in our local prison, I found that their spiritual suffering was magnified by their situation. Many of them were separated from their families by hundreds, sometimes thousands of miles. Some had family support; most had been ostracized, neglected, even consciously erased from memory by family members. All of these women were daughters, some of them mothers and grandmothers. Though disconnected, even alienated from the world, they expressed deep regret for the harm they had caused others. Like all of us, they yearned to be remembered, to believe their lives mattered, to make a positive contribution that would outlive them.

One inmate, Cindy, came to the legacy circle looking despondent. She'd heard her granddaughter cooing while talking long distance with her daughter, and she despaired of ever seeing or holding the child. Another inmate, Pat, said that she, too, had a granddaughter whom she'd never seen. She had vowed to write at least one sentence to the child every day. On days when she could think of nothing special to say, she would look out the window, return to her paper, and write, "My darling Sophia, the grass is very green." She wanted Sophia to know that her grandmother thought about her every day of her life. Upon hearing this story, Cindy's face brightened with hope. She said, "I can do that. I will do that! Thanks, Pat."

In addition to helping others write their legacies, more and more women are documenting the history of a meaningful institution – their place of worship, the town square, their mother's elementary school, an old theater. For example, members of a faith community will sometimes join together to record the formation and history of their church, synagogue, or mosque, gathering stories about the families who have worshiped there. They document unique holiday traditions as well as birth, death, marriage, and coming-of-age rituals. In so doing they leave a valuable legacy, deepening their community's roots, preserving its traditions, and enriching its families. Many years from now, when women who are planning weddings or funerals read about the ceremonies of previous congregants, their place of worship will seem more than a building – it will be a vessel of family memories as documented by its women.

Legacies can be documented for any institution. For example, creative high school teachers in a small Wisconsin town turned a modest history project into a long-lasting tribute to their community. Students were assigned to interview people over seventy about life in the first half of the twentieth century. While the teachers had hoped the project would help students connect with their heritage, open a dialogue with their elders, and deepen their sense of belonging, the

Harvest the meaning of life and pass it down to the next generation through stories.
– Joan Borysenko

An ethical commitment to the species and to the planet starts from the local turf, the air and the water.
– Mary Catherine Bateson

Grandma Bertha Davis

You never came to our house.
Every Sunday afternoon from two to three-thirty
we'd go to yours.

The same smells crept into our noses
each week
and lingered there
for hours after we left.
Gas from the stove invaded our senses
followed by the faint smell of urine
that was your perfume.
The air was warm and stuffy
like a home for the aged.
Leftover burnt coffee grounds
were still in the saucepan on the stove
from lunch.

On every windowsill, blue Mason jars
filled with liquid
tried to birth orange and grapefruit seeds
into green, leafy plants.
Lacking sunlight
they withered and hung drooping,
pale-green spindles like after the first frost.

In the bathroom
all lined in a row
on the toilet tank top
were massive jars of Vaseline.
Deep grooves were dug
by fingers grasping for
salve
hoping to smooth the roughness.

Big Russian peasant woman,
speaker of a foreign language,
your eyes were small and black,
like bats in the night.
"Speak up," you'd shout.
We'd run and hide
behind familiar skirts.
Large, crippled hands,
high, black-leather laced bunion shoes,
you were imprisoned in your body.

Seated on the big, overstuffed horsehair couch,
avoiding springs poking into our buttocks,
little feet swinging,
eyes downcast,
we'd wait.
Endless moments of silence
except for the tuneless hum
that escaped your throat
like a chant
with its own regular monotonous rhythm –
lullaby never sung, love song pinched in your cords.
Finally the time would come.
Grasping our little warm, smooth hands
in your big gnarled fingers
you placed the eagerly awaited coins in our palms
and, ever so gently, closed our hands and yours over them,
leaving your imprint upon us.
We hurried downstairs to the drugstore
for our reward.

– Sandy Swirnoff

results exceeded all expectations. The students' fascinating collection of tales and photos was published fifteen years later as *Echoes of Portage County Past: An Oral History: 1900–1950,* by the county historical society. A tribute to the roots of rural and small-town Midwesterners, the book captured the flavor of immigration, the Great Depression, and life during World Wars I and II. The 180 vignettes painted a picture of diverse backgrounds, traditions, and ethnicities, all successfully integrated into this small community.

One student, Jodi Patoka, wrote about her great-aunt's 1917 wedding: "She married . . . at St. Adalbert's Church. . . . [T]he families . . . showed up at the wedding with their horse and buggy. . . . A breakfast started out the day. The ceremony, dinner and supper followed after it. Dancing was in a tent in the afternoon and the reception lasted until midnight. The band was . . . a concertina, violin and drums. The music was mainly polkas or hop waltz. A bridal dance was done instead of giving wedding gifts. A person would put a dollar in a basket and they would get to dance with the bride. The next day they had a Polish get-together. The immediate family gathered to eat the leftover food from the wedding."

This simple description, written by a teenager, evokes a sense of family, faith, community, tradition. Through it we hear the music, taste the food, and witness the rituals of a 1917 Polish-American wedding. Such documentation preserves a community's roots, which are too often buried with the passage of time, and allows the future to remain firmly grounded in the past. It is a legacy, a gift of belonging to family and community.

For information on how to help others document their legacies, see "Facilitating Legacy Circles" on page 255.

REFLECTION AND WRITING

Whether they realize it or not, many women have already documented the lives of others or captured the history of an important institution. The family photographer has stored decades of history in her photo album. The quilter might have stitched together swatches of her grandmothers' dresses, her mother's baby blanket, and her great-aunt's handmade pillowcases. The poet may have written a series on the old, overgrown cemetery at the edge of town.

~ *Part 1*   *(25 to 60 minutes)*

Reflect on contributions you have made to historical preservation, no matter how small or unusual. Write about these contributions to clarify their historical, ethnic, and family value. Be sure to name the people who should receive your creations after you are gone. You may wish to include this documentation in your spiritual-ethical will.

~ *Part 2*   *(60 minutes)*

Helping others to preserve and pass on their histories is simply an extension of your own legacy work. It is a significant gift to the future, to the other person, and to you. If you wish to document another person's legacy, consider these suggestions:

- Write a few sentences about why or how this person's history and legacy will be valuable to future generations.
- Examine the differences between writing to preserve and pass on your own history and writing for and with another person. Explore your motivation, goals, and hopes for this endeavor. Also consider who the other person is: his or her circumstances, age, health, cognitive state, and level of trust in your relationship. All these and more will determine the outcome of your efforts.
- Write a vignette or an anecdote about this person. You may share it as a way to introduce your wish to document his or her values and wisdom.

- Review the questioning technique used to document the legacies of our feminine ancestors (see chapter 3). Prepare a list of questions to structure what you want to preserve and pass on. Topics might include immigration and settlement stories, memories from the "old country," stories of the family homestead, family traditions and special occasions, births, marriages, deaths, significant transitions, spiritual beliefs and experiences, important life lessons and values, specific messages for loved ones, and preferences related to death and dying. The other person may wish to add or delete items from your list.
- Prioritize your list. You may begin with the simplest or most important topics, or you might proceed chronologically. Include the other person when assigning priorities. The two of you may decide to audiotape or videotape your time together, either to assist your writing or to include as part of your gift to future generations.
- Write a blessing to acknowledge the sacred nature of this work. You may want to repeat this blessing to begin each meeting.
- Establish a timeline and action plan.

~ *Part 3*   *(30 to 60 minutes)*

If you wish to preserve the history and traditions of an institution or community, write at least one sentence articulating your decision and commitment. Because most preservation projects are best done in concert with others, your next step is to "call a circle" of interested women. A circle includes two or more women.

- The circle's first task is to agree on goals and define the breadth of the project. Preserving the marriage traditions practiced in your local house of worship, for example, is less complicated than preserving the history of your hometown. You may choose to begin simply, taking on more work as you go.
- Some work is best done individually, in pairs, or by the entire circle. Decide how to delegate tasks, allowing each woman to define her participation by her skills, interests, and time available. Once you've

implemented your plans, support each other's progress and assist one another in problem solving.

- Keep a written record of your goals, division of labor, action plan, and timeline.
- Begin each meeting with a blessing to recognize the sacred nature of your work together. Take time to celebrate as you accomplish your goals.
- Record your individual experiences and share your thoughts and feelings. Because of the emotional and time commitments, begin a second project only after you have completed the first community legacy.

Artistic Legacies

Having faithfully completed the exercises in this book, you are now the proud owner of a journal full of thoughts and feelings, values and stories, beliefs and blessings. But perhaps your legacy is best expressed in other ways. If you are a visual artist, storyteller, craft worker, photographer, or poet, for example, you might bring an artistic component to your spiritual-ethical will.

Take Sandy, a fifty-three-year-old mother of six. Sandy is serving a twenty-year sentence at a women's prison, but her legacy is steeped in love. Every day, Sandy crochets dolls for children without families. The dolls are given annually to the children at a local orphanage. In her spiritual-ethical will, Sandy writes, "My doll was my best friend. She gave me love, hugs; she was there for me. A part of me died when I had to burn my doll. (My mom thought at age ten I was too old for a doll.) I was not pretty or smart. That doll was my only friend. That's why I crochet dolls now, to help children find a friend with a doll of their own. Knowing there are many people I've hurt, to be able to do something good for people makes me feel alive inside."

To be able to give, one has to possess, and we possess no other life, no other living sap, than the treasures stored up from the past and digested, assimilated and created afresh by us.
– Simone Weil

Susan Richards, a visual artist, has expressed her legacy through a multimedia collage. Its title, *Kaddish,* refers to the Hebrew prayer said annually in remembrance of the dead. Susan explains her art in her spiritual-ethical will: "As I age, I have an increasing sense of my own mortality, of being a link in a chain of generations. This mixed-media piece includes a photo-transparency of my grandmother, my own footprint from my birth certificate, my mother's handwriting, and fragments of the Kaddish. The garter, rubber glove, and sewing items suggest that this is a Kaddish for women. In the course of doing this piece, I realized how important it is to me that my descendants some-day say Kaddish for me. The rotary phone dial in the collage implies 'Kaddish – your dial-up connection.' "

Barbara Ottinger is a breast cancer survivor. While participating in a legacy circle, she discovered that her gift to the future extends beyond a written document. It combines her two greatest passions: flowers and photography. Because she has no children, the beneficiaries of her floral photographs include friends and extended family.

Like Barbara, Helen Redman draws on the natural world to express her unique legacy. A feminist artist and writer, Helen uses literal and metaphorical portraits to depict the special beauty, wisdom, and experience of aging women. She paints analogies between wrinkled hands and tree bark, gnarled fingers and tree roots, affectionately reaffirming the Crone not as a withered old woman, but as a triumphant expression of all phases of a woman's life. Weaving alternative visions of power and beauty, she examines ageism, sexism, and healthcare. She writes that the purpose of her paintings is to transform the negative and distorted images of postmenopausal women that abound in the popular media.

When fiber and bead artist Sandy Swirnoff found a box of fading family photographs, she felt a strong urge to preserve them. Creating beaded frames was a step in reconnecting with her matriarchal ancestors.

When the shriveled skin of the ordinary is stuffed out with meaning, it satisfies the senses amazingly.
– Virginia Woolf

To create one's world in any of the arts takes courage.
– Georgia O'Keeffe

History is an important aspect of my work: personal history, family history, and the history of women. Within that context, I create my own story, my own unique history. As I work I imagine the many women in every culture working with similar materials for a multitude of purposes. I'm inspired by and grateful for the infinite quantity of stitches that have been sewn by generations of women. Those stitches carry within them each woman's secrets, prayers, and dreams. I am obsessed by the "stitch" and its metaphor as a "mark" to catalog time, events, and emotions. I need to follow the line of that stitch, knowing that wherever the work takes me, I will hear my own story.

– Beth Barron, fiber artist

"The photographs that spoke to me instantly were of my mother and her mother. Mom was a gentle and creative woman, full of love and encouragement . . . my artistic inspiration. Mom's frames are flowery and delicate. And Grandma was, well, a little spiky, so her image called for black points and antique buttons." These beaded frames have become a component of Sandy's legacy.

Pat Cummings' legacy takes the form of children's writing. "In 1992, I decided to write a book for my granddaughters about a contemporary grandmother, because none of the commercial books about grandmothers related in any way to my life. The result was a little story called 'My Granny Is Hip.' In the course of the writing I began to ask myself, What do I want these little girls to know? What wisdom do I have to share with them? Thus began a profound, introspective process of articulating my values — my legacy, if you will — and distilling them into a few short thoughts that would be meaningful to children.

"When my first grandson was born, I was more ambitious: I wrote a fairy tale, a book within a book called 'Quinn the Cerebral and the Book of All Wisdom.' Again, this was an opportunity to share my values and principles. 'The Book of All Wisdom' contained in the fairy tale has only four pages: 'Bring joy to those around you. Win through wit, not through force. Share your gifts. If you keep following the arrows, you will complete the circle that connects us all — the circle that is life.' At the end Quinn asks, 'Is this really all the wisdom of the world?' And Nanny answers, 'It is enough.' Whether it will be enough for my grandchildren remains to be seen. For now, I am just happy to have shared my legacy and to know that they love the stories."

REFLECTION AND WRITING *(60 minutes)*

Few of us consider ourselves artists, yet most of us have created things that are meaningful to others. Many women compile recipe books to preserve family and ethnic traditions. Others design scrapbooks or annotated family photo albums. Some women, like their mothers and grandmothers before them, do handwork – knitting, crocheting, embroidering, beading, tatting, rug hooking, weaving. Once a necessity, these crafts are now regarded as creative expressions of beauty.

To document your own artistic legacy, consider the following:

- Contemplate the things you have made. Begin by touring your home, paper and pen in hand, and note all the things you have created. Then return to your writing space and describe each item. Consider the period of your life when you made it, the materials you used, its purpose, and what you like about it.

- Review your list to consider which of your works you would like to pass on, and to whom. Write the name of each recipient next to the appropriate item on your list.

- Write about the history and meaning of each creation, explaining why you have made it a part of your legacy. (I inherited a hand-crocheted afghan, given to my mother as a wedding gift. It's beautiful, but I don't know who made it. Perhaps it was crocheted by my Gramma Minnie. Passing it down to my daughter is less meaningful because it will come to her without a story.) Include this writing, along with a list of your creations and their recipients, in your spiritual-ethical will. You might also tag each article to prevent confusion after you're gone.

Loss

She was dying. They had said that it could be any time. Already her feet had started to turn blue. Her heart was giving out. Each breath was shallow, no longer replenishing her frail body. Her face was colorless, her skin transparent, but there was still beauty in her eyes, just a touch of the sparkle that used to light her entire face. She had had a way of quivering when she spoke of her convictions, her head tipped upward, her eyes glistening, her face trembling, but now there was so little strength.

Her only son was at her bedside, holding her hand. They had been close over the years. She loved him deeply. She had so valued their times together, their phone calls, and all of the sharing. When the focus of his life shifted toward wife and children, there had been less time for their connection. She had accepted this change and had been renewed and energized by her precious grandchildren.

He sat in silence. Even with her eyes closed, he knew she wasn't asleep. He could feel her thoughts moving in the air. Suddenly he felt a change. He could feel a different energy in her hand. Her body began to tighten. She opened her eyes. At first she seemed to look at him, through him, to her life. Then she began to speak, quite slowly.

"Wind . . . stars. I was always proud that I could tell you the stories of the stars . . . the beautiful white trillium . . . green . . . green fields."

He knew to remain silent. Being present was enough. He listened. The words were often punctuated by a gasping for breath. Suddenly her thoughts seemed to become more intelligible, almost gaining strength by their content.

Her face went tight again as she started speaking faster. "You know how much I loved you, always, don't you?" She struggled to explain, leaning forward for emphasis. "I never was sure you knew I loved you just because of who you are. I loved you when you weren't at your best, when you were struggling. I didn't need you to be a star, the best." She paused and seemed to be remembering further back. Very quietly and slowly she spoke again. "I wasn't loved like that." And then she repeated, looking directly at him, "I hope you really know I loved you, all of you."

This time, he nodded. But still he remained silent. It was not time for his words.

"Josh, Josh," she said, "I have so many things still to tell you." There was intensity again, and then suddenly the tempo of her words began to shift. And from some faraway place came her words. Slowly, with clear deliberation and yet with softness, she began, "May your search never keep you from knowing that truth changes." She paused, feeling the need to explain more. "I don't think we ever really figure it out. I have never found many permanent truths, but I never regretted the search."

More poured out. "May you always find a place in your life for your spiritual voices. I never felt whole when my soul wasn't awakened." She paused, reflecting on her words. "I think raising a child is a spiritual experience. I gave everything that I had to give, but the outcome was not in my hands." Then she smiled, "But you have been quite wonderful.

"May you always be willing to share your feelings and thoughts with others. I think I betrayed myself when I kept myself hidden. Sometimes it hurt to share, but it also hurt not to."

Her words seemed to roll out. "Growth came to me from so many places in my life." She paused, looking for those special words again. "May you find new learning in all your experiences.

"May you always make space for acts of kindness. It is a huge gift to others, way beyond anything we can imagine."

She was talking to him in a different way than he had ever heard before. Her words floated; they were not heavy, like advice. She seemed to be passing on her wisdom. She began again. "May the little things in life always have value to you. Do you remember how special it was when we splurged on bakery cookies or went out for ice cream to the special ice cream store?

"May your laughter grow." She smiled with a half-laugh. "That wasn't always easy, for me with my overseriousness, but I got better." A pause again. "I have come to see laughter a bit like a miracle. With laughter, the whole mood changes.

"May you find value and meaning in nature." He could feel her remembering. "There is so much to think about – why the deer came through our backyard or the owl appeared in the afternoon light. These sights have always lifted me and taught me. I have often pondered why it was a windy day when my mother died."

The wisdom kept pouring out. He couldn't help wondering if she had written out some of her words beforehand. "May there come a time when the critical voice that is inside all of us can be quiet inside you." He could see her feeling the need to explain more. "It has been my life's struggle to accept myself as I am, that I am not as good and as perfect as I would like to be. My critical voices have brought me a lot of pain, getting in the way of my living joyfully and fully." He could feel a deep integrity to her words. Her voice lightened as she continued. "It helped when I came to see my own special gifts, my own uniqueness. I see imperfections more as humanness now."

She paused again, starting a new direction.

"Listening is one of the greatest gifts to give to others and yourself. When I have been truly listened to, it has allowed me to feel loved and valued. It is hard to be a good listener. When I have listened to others, I am startled at how much I hear and how much more people will say." He hoped he was listening and taking all of this in.

It seemed as if she could go on forever, but suddenly she stopped. There was silence, leaving again only the sound of shallow breathing. For a moment he feared it was over. Then some words again. "Walking on the beach . . . those pelicans . . . the seagulls." She twisted slightly in bed. "Big white snowflakes . . . deer tracks." She seemed to be moving through the seasons. "Those yellow warblers in the spring . . ." she trailed off. More silence. And then he knew it was over. She had finished.

– Susan Eastman Tilsch

*May the blessings of
your legacy live beyond
your given days.*

CHAPTER TWELVE

Finishing Your
Spiritual-Ethical Will

There is no one right way to preserve your legacy. You may decide to publish a small book, write a one-page letter for each of your children or grandchildren, or record your words on audio or videotape. Visual artists might also paint, print, or sculpt their legacies; craftswomen may weave their legacies into quilts, rugs, wall hangings, or baskets; gardeners will literally seed the future, planting and tending trees and other perennials. Women who leave alternative legacies often complete a written legacy as well, explaining their gifts to future generations.

No matter what forms you choose for your spiritual-ethical will – whether audio, video, stitchery, paintings, gardening, poetry, letters, creative writing, or annotated photographs – this chapter offers techniques to help you finish and communicate your legacy. Once you decide how to organize, edit, and preserve your written document, you'll consider how best to celebrate its completion, prepare recipients, and present your legacy.

Many legacy writers find it difficult to complete this stage of their work. Fatigue, anxiety, fear, shyness, perfectionism, procrastination – any of these may delay or prevent the completion of your spiritual-ethical will. It's important, therefore, to promise yourself to keep up the momentum and see your work through to the end.

Commitment

Is your writing finished? If not, when do you expect to complete it? It would be a shame to get bogged down now, after such a profound effort. Whether you give yourself a week, a month, or a year, it's important to commit to your goal.

"Finishing" your spiritual-ethical will may mean finalizing the document. If you have tasted your mortality through illness, personal transition, or a devastating world event, you may feel pressed to complete this writing. Many women, however, prefer to finish the document for now, updating it annually or whenever life events demand.

At this stage in your legacy work, you may encounter any number of obstacles to finishing your document. Perhaps the most common is the strong sense of vulnerability that comes with sharing a spiritual-ethical will. After all, the written word is a powerful tool, and many women are fearful of displaying their power. Some are afraid of being dismissed or ridiculed; others fear they will endanger themselves if they stand tall and speak what they believe. Still others worry that they will be rejected and end up alone. Fear of our own power has made women smaller and less effective than we have the potential to be. Until we acknowledge our fears and gather our strength, we may find ourselves trapped in an endless cycle of procrastination, never completing our legacies.

Not to reveal

yourself to another

is never to believe the real

you is worth loving.

– Gail Whiting

REFLECTION AND WRITING

~ *Part 1*   *(30 minutes)*

Write about the variables in your life that might distract or prevent you from finishing your work. How will you overcome these obstacles? Remember that friends, family, and the women in your legacy circle can offer immeasurable support and encouragement. If you're working alone, go to www.womenslegacies.com for support. The Interactive Connections page offers readers the opportunity to ask specific questions and express concerns about completing their legacies.

~ *Part 2*   *(no time limit)*

To underscore your commitment to finish your spiritual-ethical will, sign the contract below.

I, _____, will complete the

writing and preparation of my spiritual-ethical will by _____ (name a

specific date). Further, I promise to honor myself, my work, and those I love by presenting

my legacy document to _____ on the occasion of

_____ in the year 20_____.

Understanding that my spiritual-ethical will may raise or reopen emotional family

issues, I vow to practice quality self-care and to seek support with a confidante, my legacy

circle, or a trusted professional as needed.

Signature _____

Date _____

Organizing Your Spiritual-Ethical Will

You are now ready to piece together your written document, deciding which of your writings are appropriate to include in your legacy. This legacy will be unlike any other. There is no one right way to organize so personal a document; there is only your way. "[A]n ethical will reflects the passions and concerns of the writer," says Deborah Berkowits Litwak of the National Multiple Sclerosis Society. "It is our responsibility to share our values, dreams and wishes with our children . . . complete with formative life events, important lessons learned, stories to be shared, a definition of success, and a message to [our family]." But legacy writing fulfills many personal needs as well: to express who we are, to have our lives and values witnessed by others, to be remembered. Our legacy documents will show that we made a difference: our lives had meaning, and the world is a better place for our having been here.

Legacies also bind future generations to the past by honoring those who have gone before us. As Elie Wiesel passionately explains in his memoir *All Rivers Run to the Sea,* "I wrote to testify, to stop the dead from dying, to justify my own survival. I wrote to speak to those who were gone. As long as I spoke to them, they would live on, at least in my memory." Many women have equally crucial reasons for writing about the past: to respect and memorialize those who may not otherwise be remembered; to testify about abuse and maltreatment in order to heal; to give shape, dimension, and life to larger cultural and historical moments. Yet, as we determine what to include in our legacies, we must also consider the needs of loved ones and the members of our communities. How will our spiritual-ethical wills affect them?

In *The Bridges of Madison County,* children who open a trunk after their mother's death find the story of her fiery love affair with an itinerant photographer. Their grief over losing a mother is complicated by

Why does anybody tell a story? It does indeed have something to do with faith, faith that the universe has meaning, that our little human lives are not irrelevant, that what we choose or say or do matters, matters cosmically.

– Madeleine L'Engle

a legacy document exposing long-held secrets. What might have happened if the mother had shared her secrets while she was alive, giving her children the opportunity to react, ask questions, express their feelings, and discuss the secrets' implications? This brings up an ethical question that every legacy writer must consider: how will you balance your need to be known and understood with the potential harm this might cause to those you love?

Remember, words can and do harm people every day, and the written word is especially powerful. It is important, therefore, to embrace the principle "do no harm" when preparing your spiritual-ethical will. Twelve Step wisdom teaches us to make amends directly to those we have hurt, unless doing so would harm them or others. Keep this in mind as you decide what to include in your legacy document. Though you are not responsible for how others interpret what you have written in good faith, it is your obligation to remove content that you think may be harmful to your readers.

She was just talking the way mothers will, not realizing that each word is a rock that daughters carry around ever after: a rock to build a fortress, a rock to throw at someone else, a rock to stand on while crossing rivers.

— Anne Roiphe

REFLECTION AND WRITING
~ Part 1   *(60 to 90 minutes)*

Before you begin the process of elimination, review all that you have written so far. It will help to categorize your writings using one of the models on the following pages. Feel free to amend these categories or create a whole new outline that reflects your unique life experiences. Be sure to categorize all of your work.

As you categorize your writings, you may discover that a necessary element is missing from your legacy. Take as many days as you need to fill in the gaps and right any imbalances before you move on. Remember, this is a sacred opportunity to communicate who you are, to give your wisdom and love to the future, and to ask loved ones to respect your end-of-life requests.

Model 1

Writings that:

- Tell my story, connecting me to my family and ancestors

- Transmit family history, connecting the past and future

- Define my values and wisdom

- Articulate my spiritual journey, my relationship with the Divine

- Express gratitude for blessings in my life

- Make amends or request forgiveness

- Give an account of the history of my money and "valuables," along with my reasons for bequeathing them

- State my life passions, the causes I care about, and my charitable gifts

- Explain my burial requests and how I want to be memorialized

- Describe my art, crafts, poetry, and other legacies

Model 2

I. Past
    A. My name(s)
    B. Legacies I've received
    C. Ancestral or family stories
    D. Other material from the past

II. Present
    A. Who am I, really?
    B. Mothering and sexuality
    C. My spiritual story and development
    D. Other material from the present

III. Future
    A. My values
    B. Instructions and blessings
    C. Letters to loved ones
    D. Personal possessions I want to pass on
    E. Financial gifts to family and others
    F. Preferences for death and dying
    G. Other legacies I will leave

~ *Part 2* *(no time limit)*

Write about your specific reasons for sharing your legacy. What do you want your legacy to accomplish? How will you ensure that your words will "do no harm"? Take as many days as you need to clarify your purpose, since this writing will guide the rest of your legacy work.

If you find yourself struggling with conflicting motives, write a dialogue with the dueling parts of yourself to hear all sides. Balance is your goal: your document should honor your integrity and authenticity without harming others, either dead or alive. Keep these points in mind as you choose which writings to include in your spiritual-ethical will. You will want to eliminate or revise any writings that do not align with your purpose.

~ *Part 3* *(45 to 90 minutes)*

As you determine the content of your spiritual-ethical will, consider your audience. Write about each of the concerns that influence your decision making.

- Who will receive your document?
- Will you create more than one copy or version?
- Will each person on your list get the same document, or will different people get different sections?
- Will you share your legacy with family members or friends who are estranged from you or each other?
- What parts of your legacy will go to your attorney, physician, clergy person, and other professionals?
- With which organizations or communities do you want to share your legacy (a historical society, library, faith community, genealogical society, or ethnic group)?

When determining which writings to include, reflect on how you can best communicate your legacy to each recipient. Some recipients need only receive a portion of your document, and certain portions will require a more formal presentation than others. For example, if you are making a charitable bequest, you might share with the organization only the documentation of your financial legacy, perhaps attaching a note about the purpose of your gift, the history and meaning of your connection with the organization, and how you hope the money will be used. You may want to give copies of these and other financial documents to family members, along with your last will and testament.

Your advance healthcare directive and related documents must go to the appropriate professionals, but it's a good idea to share copies with your family as well. Communicating these decisions is essential for your peace of mind and theirs.

Professionals, with the possible exception of clergy, have no need for your funeral and burial requests if your loved ones have or know where to find your written document.

How to Edit and Preserve Your Legacy

You've selected the writings to include in your legacy. Now what? You don't need to be a professional writer or editor to complete your spiritual-ethical will. Your goal is to bless those you love and say simply and beautifully who you are, what you value, and how you want to be remembered. With a few easy techniques, you can transform your raw material into a meaningful, long-lasting gift.

This editing is not about perfecting for publication, it's about polishing for presentation. You are going to decide what to change in your document and what to retain. Six vital tips will make your spiritual-ethical will the best it can be: avoid comparing your work, determine what's "interesting," find the right words, be specific, read aloud, and preserve your legacy.

When I write, I have a real existence that is proper to the activity of writing — an existence that takes place midway between me and the sphere of artifice, art, pure language.

– Eva Hoffman

AVOID COMPARING YOUR WORK

Don't compare your writing to that of professionals or the women in your legacy circle. This is a slippery slope that ends in self-criticism, worry, and loss of joy. Spiritual-ethical wills are unique to their writers in every way; like apples and oranges, they are impossible to compare.

In a legacy circle at a women's prison, Pat emerged as a natural, artful, and prolific writer. Her ability to articulate her beliefs, as well as her vivid expressions of feeling, touched us all. At first, the other women were reticent to share their writings, especially those who had less education than Pat or whose primary language wasn't English. They soon recognized, however, that each of them had something unique and valuable to express. In that difficult and depressing prison setting, these women felt fortunate to receive the gift of Pat's writing, and they came to see it as no more valuable than their own. Pat was generous, too, always a responsive and appreciative listener. A bond of trust and respect was formed, and every woman shared her writing on at least one occasion.

DETERMINE WHAT'S INTERESTING

Editing your legacy document means, in part, deciding which portions of your writing are interesting. As you read through the components of your legacy, put your audience out of your mind for a moment and ask yourself: Which details matter most to me? Which sections make my life experiences come alive? What parts of the writing are evocative? If there are sections that bore you, feel irrelevant, or plod along too slowly, you might consider taking them out or finding ways to make them vivid.

Now think of your audience. Imagine your future relatives reading your spiritual-ethical will in the twenty-second century. How might they respond? If just one person better understands the time in which you lived, if one long-estranged relationship is redeemed, if one reader

Women's written words will change the culture.

– Joan Drury

There are stories that never, never die, that are carried like seed into a new country, are told to you and me and make in us new and lasting strengths.

– Meridel le Sueur

experiences a family, ethnic, tribal, or historical connection, then your work qualifies as "interesting" and all your efforts will have been worth it.

FIND THE RIGHT WORDS

Don't hesitate to rework portions of your legacy. If you write what you mean and mean what you write, you're more likely to choose words that communicate your message clearly and vividly. When a word doesn't quite give the nuance or flavor that you want to convey, look to your dictionary, Rodale's *The Synonym Finder,* or *Roget's International Thesaurus* for help.

Sometimes a dramatic word that grabs attention is just what you want. Julia Cameron, for example, writes about a young woman whose prose "snorts with spirit." Patricia Hampl recalls feelings "stapled" by the glance of a bank teller in Italy. With one carefully chosen word, each of these authors created an arresting, dynamic image for the reader.

The best way to find the right words, of course, is through reading. Whether in books, magazines, or billboards, it is marvelous to stumble on that one perfect word. And sometimes, words arrive as intuitive gifts. Though you may not even know what they mean until you look them up in the dictionary, they turn out to be just the right words to describe your experience. Be on the lookout for words that match your personality as well as your vocabulary.

Be on the alert to find appropriate words wherever you read, but before you use them be sure they are congruous when side by side with the words of your own vocabulary.

– Dorothea Brande

BE SPECIFIC

As you edit your writing, focus on painting a picture with words. Try to use specific details that evoke the senses. The more specific you can be, the more likely your writing is to find its way into readers' hearts. On the following page is a letter from my cousin Milton. Notice the details in the letter, how his words appeal to the senses and draw the reader in.

I, lion, give you my roar, the voice to speak out and be heard.

– Joanna Macy

You can imagine my emotions when I opened your letter and the picture of Gramma Minnie fell out. Who is that woman? The face was so familiar. I looked at the picture closely, and then I remembered. I had never seen a picture of her before, and the last time I saw her was in the 1950s. The memories flooded back.

When I look back to the time when I was a small child (between 1937 and 1940), I always think of Gramma. I remember telling her a fantastic story about how I had spent the previous day – of course, it was pure fantasy – and her chasing me around the table where she prepared the challah, waving a ladle, yelling "little liar, little liar!" And I ran screaming, running away from her, my little legs pumping like mad. The two of us laughing, and her hugging me. God, I loved that woman.

Gramma's house was filled with the most unusual smells. I never knew them elsewhere. There is a certain smell of a kind of kuchen with prunes and nuts and poppy seeds, all of these between layers of dough; of oxtail soup; blintzes. For some reason, I remember the smell of roasted carrots so distinctly. Years later, when my daughter Sarah was small, she, her mother, and I baked that sort of kuchen and challah and rye bread. It wasn't until I began to write this letter that I realized I was trying to create for my daughter some of the happiness of my own childhood by recreating times I had with Gramma.

She came to California to stay with us for a while when I was a teenager, and I had the pleasure of seeing her again. I very well remember her. She must have been in her seventies when she crossed the country to visit her daughter and her children. No, she was not a difficult woman. She was not vain. She was a completely independent, mature person. Today her independence would not seem unusual.

– Milton Lieberman

READ ALOUD

After you have edited your document, set the writing aside for a while. When you come back to it, read it aloud to the women in your legacy circle, a trusted friend, or a mirror. There's no easier way to decide on punctuation. You will hear your voice falling slightly, suggesting a comma. When your voice comes to a complete stop, this is a clue that you need end punctuation.

Listen as you read. Does it read smoothly? Does your writing clearly communicate your meaning? Does it make sense? Have you offered specific details to bring the page to life? What is the general tone of the writing? Listen especially for anger, resentment, or blame, and remember your intention to do no harm. Reading aloud may also bring up additional memories, thoughts, and feelings, prompting you to add one more thing to your spiritual-ethical will.

PRESERVE YOUR LEGACY

Is your spiritual-ethical will a document? Is it a pamphlet or book? Should it have a cover? What qualities do you want to express with your design and format? Should your spiritual-ethical will look elegant, beautiful, simple, or ornate? Will you communicate parts of your legacy visually, orally, or using other media?

Women who are artistic, love crafts, or have an eye for beautiful textures and patterns will particularly enjoy the preservation aspect of their legacy work. Acid-free and archival papers are inexpensive, and there are many beautiful folders, notebooks, and containers to suit most tastes and budgets. For the computer literate, desktop publishing programs allow attractive, personalized designs complete with electronically scanned photographs and color graphics. We can preserve text, photos, graphics, and even audio and video messages on CD and DVD.

The universe is made of stories, not of atoms.
– Muriel Rukeyser

Creativity is inventing, experimenting, growing, taking risks, breaking rules, making mistakes, and having fun.
– Mary Lou Cook

There is not one big cosmic
meaning for all, there is only
the meaning we each give to
our life, an individual
meaning, an individual plot,
like an individual novel, a
book for each person.
– Anaïs Nin

Some women feel that modern technology is too impersonal to convey the uniqueness of their legacy. To preserve the intimacy of the spiritual-ethical will, many women prefer to write it longhand. Their handwriting then becomes another aspect of the document to be preserved and passed down, much like those faded notes written in the margins of our grandmothers' cookbooks. If your legacy is lengthy, you may want to handwrite some components while generating others on a computer or typewriter. Jeanne Bearmon, for example, wrote this brief letter in her own hand to accompany individual picture albums she created for each of her children:

To my treasured children,

More than material things already gifted, and beyond that which is bequeathed in my last will and testament, I hope I have given you a love of your faith, a trust in God, and a devotion to family, fairness, and peace. These are among the precious jewels that will enrich your life with vitality and wonder.

I hope you will enjoy good health, good humor, and well-being.

I hope you will use yourself with passion and compassion.

I wish you a life lived with love, courage, and fantasy. Explore, dream, and discover!

Your loving mom

All acts of memory are to
some extent imaginative....
It is only through the efforts
of imagination and memory
that the shadows can be made
to speak.
– Eva Hoffman

If you're not sure how you want to preserve your legacy, ask for help. Discuss design ideas with the women in your legacy circle, or take a friend shopping at your local art store. If you are working alone, you can seek encouragement and support through the Interactive Connections page at www.womenslegacies.com. If you're working in a legacy circle, you may want to plan regular meetings to support the editing and presentation process. You might also exchange telephone numbers and email addresses so you can get in touch when you need understanding.

Legacy circle participants may wish to create a completion ritual, coming together to celebrate each woman as she finishes her document. The ritual may include food, dance, drums, songs, and blessings. Each woman honored may use this ritual as a practice run for presenting her finished document.

Presenting Your Legacy

Some women present their documents when they complete their spiritual-ethical wills, others wait for a particularly meaningful event, such as a birthday, holiday, or other special occasion. After the formal presentation, many women choose to update their documents with annual letters to each recipient.

Consider the best time to present your spiritual-ethical will. Does your health or age affect your plan? Might you give some sections now and some later? Some while you are alive and others after your death? How will you ensure that your loved ones receive your legacy if something unexpected happens to you?

When ninety-two-year-old Irene lay dying in the spring of 2000, she asked her children to empty her safe-deposit box. In it they found a letter she'd written in October 1981:

> My dearest children:
> No one knows how much time God has allotted to them, and I can't leave you without a final word. I was blessed with a very good life – good friends, good health, a loving husband, wonderful children and grandchildren – so do not mourn my passing beyond showing your respect for me. The important thing is how you treated me when I was alive – and that you couldn't have done better. . . .
> I love you all and hope that you have many happy years with your families and friends, and that you are able to realize all your hopes and dreams.

Irene's children drew great comfort from this letter. She had blessed them first with her hopes for their future, and again in asking them not to mourn her unduly. Long before her death, Irene had contemplated the end of life, consciously leaving a legacy of peace and serenity for her children.

If you choose to share all or part of your legacy after your death, be sure to leave detailed instructions so recipients will know where to find your document. Presenting your legacy while you're still living, however, requires a more elaborate plan. You don't want to drop your legacy without warning at a family picnic or holiday dinner. How, then, will you prepare your recipients? Will you mail them your spiritual-ethical will, or present it in person? Do you want to be there while your loved ones read it? Are you open to discussing the content and hearing how others feel about what you wrote?

Reflect on the possible consequences of sharing your legacy. How do you imagine loved ones will respond to this gift? How would you have responded if your parents or ancestors had left you this legacy? What might happen to you, your recipients, or your relationships after you share your spiritual-ethical will? Do these thoughts tilt the scale toward waiting until your death? What are possible resolutions for these difficulties? Would it help to discuss your concerns with a friend or the women in your legacy circle? In the end, you cannot control how your gift will be received. If you're as sure as you can be that what you've written is truthful, ethical, and loving, you must be willing to let go of the results.

REFLECTION AND WRITING   *(20 to 60 minutes)*

Mary O'Brien Tyrrell writes memoirs for the elderly. She concludes each project by helping her client design a presentation ritual, which often includes food and music. In small towns, the whole community may be invited to join the festivities, and copies of the memoir are sometimes given to the local historical society, library, or religious center.

Many legacy writers create a ritual – or a series of rituals – to commemorate the presentation of their spiritual-ethical will. Though each ritual is unique, it will generally involve a gathering of loved ones along with appropriate ethnic or spiritual traditions. The celebration is sometimes recorded to memorialize the event and permit absent family members to be included.

In this exercise, you will discover your own unique way of presenting your spiritual-ethical will to loved ones. To prepare for this visualization, review your list of recipients as well as the contract you signed at the beginning of this chapter. If you've been thinking about how to present your completed spiritual-ethical will, gather those thoughts now.

If you are working in a legacy circle, you may want to record the following directions so all participants can visualize simultaneously. If you're working alone, you might record them yourself or ask someone else to read them to you.

> *When you are ready to begin, arrange yourself so you are comfortable where you are sitting. Close your eyes and focus your attention on your breath, following its natural rhythm . . . in . . . and out. Notice that with each inhalation you feel more centered and relaxed, and with each exhalation you let go of any distractions around you. . . .*
>
> *Now imagine that you are a woman who enjoys people and celebrations, and that you have planned this special occasion to present your legacy to those you love. If a large group would be uncomfortable or is not your style, imagine that this is the first in a series of small gatherings. Maybe you've made tea and scones for the occasion, or arranged an intimate dinner to precede the presentation of your legacy gift. Perhaps you've invited loved ones to gather outdoors in your garden or in your favorite serene setting. You might offer your legacy as part of a special birthday celebration or holiday, like Thanksgiving.*
>
> *Take a moment to visualize your own presentation plan, time, and space. . . .*
> *Now, in your mind's eye, see yourself entering this space with your spiritual-*

ethical will. No one has arrived yet, and you still have time to make sure every-thing you want is here. . . . Notice how you look, how you are dressed . . . the physical arrangements you have put in place. . . . See yourself lighting the room, perhaps with candles . . . making an adjustment to your favorite flowers . . . put-ting the final touches on the table . . . turning on the music you have chosen for the background. . . .

Observe how you feel as the moment arrives. . . . You may experience some trepidation or doubt — that's natural — but mostly you feel calm and clear, authentic and dignified. Take a few deep and full breaths. . . . This day is the culmination of your great effort, your thinking and feeling, writing and plan-ning, preparing and anticipating. . . .

Now, imagine that everyone has arrived. You begin with a planned ritual . . . perhaps a prayer or blessing. . . . You describe what led up to this day, and then you present your legacy. See each person receiving this legacy — an expression of your love. . . . Be aware of their responses and of the significant precedent you have set. Perhaps your loved ones will decide to pass their own legacies, wisdom, and love down through the generations.

Experience this effect now, in this moment . . . imagine that you can see beyond this time and space into the future. . . . Be aware of the influence your legacy will have twenty, fifty, or a hundred years from now. Perhaps you see a light shining . . . or you sense a greater respect for values and ethics . . . or you feel love increasing as human souls connect . . . or you sense communities nurtur-ing and protecting the earth. . . . See the cumulative impact of women's spiritual-ethical wills . . . of women finding their voices and courage, writing their values, their histories, their stories, their blessings, their wisdom, their love. . . .

Now, open your eyes and begin to write your experience. Recreate your vision as best you can, and write about the ritual you'll construct to celebrate the presen-tation of your spiritual-ethical will. Capturing these elements will allow you to plan in detail how to realize your vision. If strong emotions and tears accompany this writing, allow them. . . . Keep writing and keep breathing deeply. . . .

When you are finished, set down your writing materials and close your eyes again. Return your awareness to this time and place, focusing on your breath as you did when you began this visualization. Take as much time as you need to come back to yourself — realizing that you are living in the present moment. You are seated in the comfort of your writing space.

Open your eyes and look around, noting your surroundings. If you are alone, stand and stretch to bring yourself fully back to the present. If you are working in a legacy circle, meet at least one other woman with your eyes, maintaining the silence as each of you gathers her unique experience. Share your vision with the other women in your circle, if you choose. Listening to others will bring you fully back to the present moment while expanding your ritual ideas. Moreover, speaking or reading your plans aloud will help ground your vision in reality.

~

The beneficiaries of your spiritual-ethical will are starved in ways that they can't even imagine. Your legacy will nourish them; your words will fill the holes in their hearts and the gaps in their histories. Through your stories, they will know and remember you. Your values will encourage and inspire them in times of cynicism, alienation, and hopelessness. Your blessings will teach them love. When they are told that all truth is relative, they will find guidance in your honesty, courage, and generosity.

Although you and I may never meet, I want to express how much I appreciate your work, how grateful I am for having walked this path with you. Congratulations for honoring your promise to yourself, for finishing your spiritual-ethical will, and for presenting it to those you love as a most valuable gift to the future. May your spiritual-ethical will be an eternal link between you and those you love.

Miracles occur naturally as expressions of love. The real miracle is the love that inspires them. In this sense everything that comes from love is a miracle.

– Marianne Williamson

Bibliography

Abrahams, Israel, ed. *Hebrew Ethical Wills.* Philadelphia: Jewish Publication Society, 1926, 1954.

Allende, Isabel. *Daughter of Fortune: A Novel.* Translated by Margaret Sayers Peden. New York: HarperCollins, 1999.

Allison, Dorothy. *Two or Three Things I Know.* New York: Penguin Group, Dutton, 1995.

Anderson, Sherry P., and Patricia Hopkins. *The Feminine Face of God.* New York: Bantam, 1991.

Angelou, Maya. *On the Pulse of Morning.* New York: Random House, 1993.

Assagioli, Roberto. *The Act of Will.* New York: Viking Press, 1973.

——. *Psychosynthesis: A Manual of Principles and Techniques.* New York: Penguin Books, 1965.

Austen, Hallie Iglehart. *The Heart of the Goddess: Art, Myth and Meditations of the World's Sacred Feminine.* Berkeley, Calif.: Wingbow Press, 1991.

Bachmann, Christina, and Celina Spiegel, eds. *Out of the Garden: Women Writers on the Bible.* New York: Fawcett Columbine, 1995.

Baines, Barry K. *Ethical Wills: Putting Your Values on Paper.* San Francisco: Perseus, 2002.

Baldwin, Christina. *Calling the Circle: The First and Future Culture.* New York: Swan, Raven, and Company, 1994.

———. *Life's Companion: Journal Writing as a Spiritual Quest.* New York: Bantam New Age, 1990.

———. *One to One: Self-Understanding through Journal Writing.* New York: M. Evans and Company, 1976.

Bancroft, Ann. *Weavers of Wisdom: Women Mystics of the Twentieth Century.* London: Arkana, 1989.

Barrington, Judith. *Writing the Memoir: From Truth to Art*. Portland, Oreg.: Eighth Mountain Press, 1997.

Baskin, Judith R., ed. *Women of the Word: Jewish Women and Jewish Writing*. Detroit: Wayne State University Press, 1994.

Bass, Ellen. *The Courage to Heal*. New York: HarperCollins, 1992.

Bateson, Mary Catherine. *Composing a Life*. New York: Penguin Group, Plume, 1989.

———. *Full Circles, Overlapping Lives: Culture and Generation in Transition*. New York: Ballantine Books, 2000.

Berkeley, Ellen Perry. *At Grandmother's Table*. Minneapolis: Fairview Press, 2000.

Berrin, Susan, ed. *A Heart of Wisdom: Making the Jewish Journey from Midlife through the Elder Years*. Woodstock, Vt.: Jewish Lights Publishing, 2000.

Bianchi, Eugene C. *Aging as a Spiritual Journey*. New York: Crossroad, 1997.

Bible, Revised Edition. New York: American Bible Society, 1952.

Bolen, Jean Shinoda. *Goddesses in Older Women: Archetypes in Women over Fifty: Becoming a Juicy Crone*. New York: HarperCollins, 2001.

———. *The Millionth Circle: How to Change Ourselves and the World: The Essential Guide to Women's Circles*. Berkeley, Calif.: Conari, 1999.

Borysenko, Joan. *Pocketful of Miracles: Prayers, Meditations, and Affirmations to Nurture Your Spirit Every Day of the Year*. New York: Warner Books, 1994.

———. *A Woman's Journey to God*. New York: Riverhead, 1999.

Boss, Pauline. *Ambiguous Loss: Learning to Live with Unresolved Grief*. Cambridge, Mass.: Harvard University Press, 1999.

Boston Women's Health Book Collective. *Our Bodies, Ourselves*. New York: Simon and Schuster, 1971.

Brande, Dorothea. *Becoming a Writer.* Los Angeles: J. P. Tarcher, 1934.

Breathnach, Sarah Ban. *Hold That Thought.* New York: Warner Books, 1997.

Bridges, William. *Transitions: Making Sense of Life's Changes.* Reading, Mass.: Addison-Wesley Publishing, 1980.

Brin, Ruth F. *Harvest: Collected Poems and Prayers.* Second Edition. Duluth, Minn.: Holy Cow! Press, 1999.

Broner, E. M. *The Telling.* New York: HarperCollins, 1993.

Brown, Judith N., and Christina Baldwin. *A Second Start: A Widow's Guide to Financial Survival at a Time of Emotional Crisis.* New York: Simon and Schuster, Fireside, 1986.

Brown, Molly Young. *Growing Whole: Self-Realization on an Endangered Planet.* Center City: Hazelden; New York: HarperCollins, 1993.

———, ed. *Lighting a Candle: Quotations on the Spiritual Life.* New York: HarperCollins, 1994.

Butler, Sandra, and Barbara Rosenblum. *Cancer in Two Voices.* Duluth, Minn.: Spinsters Ink, 1991.

Cameron, Julia. *The Artist's Way: A Spiritual Path to Higher Creativity.* New York: Putnam, J. P. Tarcher, 1992.

———. *The Right to Write.* New York: Putnam, J. P. Tarcher, 1998.

Carmack, Sharon DeBartolo. *A Genealogist's Guide to Discovering Your Female Ancestors: Special Strategies for Uncovering Hard-to-Find Information about Your Female Lineage.* Cincinnati, Ohio: Betterway Books, 1998.

Chefitz, Mitchell. *The Seventh Telling: The Kabbalah of Moshe Katan.* New York: St. Martin's Press, 2001.

Chittister, Joan D. *In Search of Mary: The Woman and the Symbol.* New York: Ballantine, 1996.

———. *The Story of Ruth: Twelve Moments in Every Woman's Life.* Grand Rapids, Mich.: William B. Eerdmans Publishing, 2000.

Cohen, Norman J. *Self, Struggle and Change: Family Conflict: Stories in Genesis and Their Healing Insights for Our Lives.* Woodstock, Vt.: Jewish Lights, 1995.

Colletta, John P. *They Came in Ships.* Salt Lake City: Ancestry, 1989.

Dass, Ram, and Paul Gorman. *How Can I Help?* New York: Alfred A. Knopf, 1985.

———. *Still Here: Embracing Aging, Changing, Dying.* New York: Riverhead Books, 2000.

DeGrazia, Monica, and Emelio DeGrazia. *33 Minnesota Poets.* Minneapolis: Nodin Press, 2000.

Doerr, Harriet. *Stones for Ibarra.* New York: Penguin Books, 1978.

Echoes of Portage County Past: An Oral History: 1900–1950. Stevens Point, Wisc.: Cornerstone Press, 2001.

Edelman, Hope. *Mother of My Mother: The Intricate Bond between Generations.* New York: Dial Press, 1999.

Edelman, Marian Wright. *The Measure of Our Success: A Letter to My Children and Yours.* New York: HarperCollins, 1993.

Edgarian, Carol. *Rise the Euphrates.* New York: Random House, 1994.

Eliach, Yaffa. *There Once Was a World: A 900-Year Chronicle of the Shtetl of Eishyshok.* Boston: Little, Brown and Company, 1998.

Eskins, Blake. *A Life in Pieces: The Making and Unmaking of Binjamin Wilkomirski.* New York: W. W. Norton and Company, 2002.

Eve, Nomi. *The Family Orchard.* New York: Alfred A. Knopf, 2000.

Falk, Marcia. *The Book of Blessings.* San Francisco: HarperSanFrancisco, 1996.

Ferré, Rosario. *The House on the Lagoon.* New York: Penguin Books, 1995.

Ferrucci, Piero. *Inevitable Grace.* Los Angeles: J. P. Tarcher, 1990.

———. *What We May Be.* Los Angeles: J. P. Tarcher, 1982.

Fowler, James W. *Stages of Faith.* San Francisco: Harper and Row, 1981.

Frank, Arthur W. *The Wounded Storyteller.* Chicago: University of Chicago Press, 1995.

Frankel, Ellen. *The Five Books of Miriam.* New York: G. P. Putnam Sons, 1996.

Frankiel, Tamar. *The Voice of Sarah: Feminine Spirituality and Traditional Judaism.* San Francisco: HarperSanFrancisco, 1990.

Frankl, Viktor E. *Man's Search for Meaning.* New York: Washington Square Press, 1963.

Fremont, Helen. *After Long Silence: A Memoir.* New York: Delta, Delacorte Press, 1999.

Frymer-Kensky, Tikva. *MotherPrayer: The Pregnant Woman's Spiritual Companion.* New York: Riverhead, 1995.

Furman, Frida Kerner. *Facing the Mirror: Older Women and Beauty Shop Culture.* New York: Routledge, 1997.

Garfield, C., C. Spring, and S. Cahill. *Wisdom Circles: A Guide to Self-Discovery and Community Building in Small Groups.* New York: Hyperion, 1998.

Gilligan, Carol. *In a Different Voice.* Cambridge, Mass.: Harvard University Press, 1982.

Glückel of Hameln. *The Memoirs of Glückel of Hameln.* Translated by Marvin Lowenthal. New York: Schocken Books, 1977.

Goldberg, Natalie. *Thunder and Lightning: Cracking Open the Writer's Craft.* New York: Bantam, 2000.

———. *Wild Mind: Living the Writer's Life.* New York: Bantam, 1990.

———. *Writing Down the Bones.* Boston, Mass.: Shambhala, 1986.

Good News Bible, Catholic Study Edition. Nashville, Tenn.: Thomas Nelson Publishers, 1979.

Goode, Erica, ed. *Letters for Our Children: Fifty Americans Share Lessons in Living.* New York: Random House, 1996.

Greene, Bob, and D. G. Fulford. *To Our Children's Children: Preserving Family Histories for Generations to Come.* New York: Doubleday, 1993.

Hampl, Patricia. *I Could Tell You Stories: Sojourns in the Land of Memory.* New York: W. W. Norton, 1999.

———. *Virgin Time: In Search of the Contemplative Life.* New York: Ballantine, 1993.

Harrison, Kathryn. *The Binding Chair: Or a Visit from the Foot Emancipation Society.* New York: HarperCollins, Perennial, 2001.

Hayden, Ruth L. *How to Turn Your Money Life Around: The Money Book for Women.* Deerfield Beach, Fla.: Health Communications, 1992.

Heilbrun, Carolyn G. *Writing a Woman's Life.* New York: Ballantine Books, 1988.

Herman, Judith. *Trauma and Recovery.* New York: Basic Books, Perseus, 1997.

Heschel, Abraham Joshua. *The Sabbath: Its Meaning for Modern Man.* New York: Farrar, Straus and Giroux, 1951.

Heschel, Susannah, ed. *On Being a Jewish Feminist.* New York: Schocken Books, 1983.

Hillman, James. *The Soul's Code: In Search of Character and Calling.* New York: Random House, 1996.

Hoffman, Eva. *Lost in Translation.* New York: Penguin Books, 1990.

———. *The Secret.* Cambridge, Mass.: Public Affairs, Perseus, 2002.

———. *Shtetl: The Life and Death of a Small Town and the World of Polish Jews.* Boston: Houghton Mifflin, 1997.

Hogan, Linda. *The Book of Medicines.* Minneapolis: Coffee House Press, 1993.

———. "Making Do." From *Braided Lives: An Anthology of Multicultural American Writing.* St. Paul, Minn.: Minnesota Humanities Commission,1991.

———. *Power.* New York: W. W. Norton and Company, 1998.

Independent Sector. "Giving and Volunteering in the United States." Waldorf, Md.: Independent Sector, 2001.

Jaffe-Gill, Ellen, ed. *The Jewish Woman's Book of Wisdom.* Secaucus, N.J.: Carol Publishing Group, 1999.

Jong, Erica. *Fear of Fifty: A Midlife Memoir.* New York: HarperCollins, 1994.

Keen, Sam, and Anne Valley-Fox. *Your Mythic Journey: Finding Meaning in Your Life through Writing and Storytelling.* Los Angeles: J. P. Tarcher, 1989.

Kenney, Susan. *Sailing.* New York: Viking Penguin, 1988.

Kern, Hermann. *Through the Labyrinth: Designs and Meanings over 5000 Years.* New York: Prestel USA, 2000.

Kessel, Barbara. *Suddenly Jewish: Jews Raised As Gentiles Discover Their Jewish Roots.* Brandeis Series in American Jewish History, Culture, and Life. Waltham, Mass.: University Press of New England, Brandeis University Press, 2000.

Kingsolver, Barbara. *Pigs in Heaven.* New York: HarperCollins, 1992.

———. *Poisonwood Bible.* New York: HarperPerennial, 1999.

———. *Prodigal Summer.* New York: HarperCollins, 2000.

Kirsch, Jonathan. *The Harlot by the Side of the Road: Forbidden Tales of the Bible.* New York: Ballantine Publishing Group, 1997.

Kugelmass, Jack, and Jonathan Boyarin, eds. and trans. *From a Ruined Garden: The Memorial Books of Polish Jewry.* New York: Schocken Books, 1983.

Kushner, Harold. *Living a Life That Matters.* New York: Anchor Books, 2002.

Kushner, Lawrence. *Eyes Remade for Wonder.* Woodstock, Vt.: Jewish Lights, 1998.

Lamott, Anne. *Bird by Bird: Some Instructions on Writing and Life.* New York: Doubleday, Anchor, 1994.

Laurence, Margaret. *The Stone Angel.* Toronto: McClelland and
   Stewart, 1964.

Lear, Frances. *Lear Magazine,* April 1994.

L'Engle, Madeleine. *Herself: Reflections on a Writing Life.* Compiled by
   Carole F. Chase. Colorado Springs, Colo.: WaterBrook Press,
   Shaw Books, 2001.

———. *Mothers and Daughters.* New York: Random House,
   Gramercy Books, 1997.

———. *Two-Part Invention: The Story of a Marriage.* New York: Farrar,
   Straus and Giroux, 1988.

Lessing, Doris. *The Summer before the Dark.* New York: Vintage Books,
   1973.

Lieber, David L., ed. *Etz Hayim: Torah and Commentary.* Philadelphia:
   Jewish Publication Society, 2001.

Linn, Denise. *Sacred Legacies: Healing Your Past and Creating a Positive
   Future.* New York: Random House, Ballantine, 1998.

Litwak, Deborah Berkowits. "So That Your Values Live On."
   <www.torahayim@shamash.org> (January 2, 1999).

Luskin, Frederic. *Forgive for Good.* New York: HarperCollins, 2001.

Macy, Joanna, and Molly Young Brown. *Coming Back to Life: Practices
   to Reconnect Our Lives, Our World.* Gabriola Island, British
   Columbia: New Society Publishers, 1998.

Magee, David S., and John Ventura. *Everything Your Heirs Need to
   Know.* Chicago: Dearborn Financial Publishing, 1999.

Martz, Sandra, ed. *When I Am an Old Woman I Shall Wear Purple.*
   Watsonville, Calif.: Paper-Mâche Press, 1991.

Mascetti, Manuela Dunn, and Priya Hemenway. *Prayer Beads.* New
   York: Penguin, Viking Compass, 2001.

Maslow, Abraham H. *The Farther Reaches of Human Nature.* New
   York: Penguin Books, 1971.

Mason, Marilyn. *Intimacy.* Center City, Minn.: Hazelden, 1986.

Mazo, Julia Wolf. *The Woman Who Lost Her Names: Selected Writings by American Jewish Women*. San Francisco: Harper and Row, 1980.

McGoldrick, Monica. *You Can Go Home Again: Reconnecting with Your Family*. New York: W. W. Norton and Company, 1995.

McLeod, Judyth. *Heritage Gardening*. Sydney, Australia: Simon and Schuster, 1994.

McNaron, Toni. *I Dwell in Possibility: A Memoir*. Second Edition. New York: Feminist Press, 2001.

McPhelimy, Lynn. *In the Checklist of Life: A Working Book to Help You Live and Leave This Life!* Rockfall, Conn.: AAIP Publishing, 1997.

"Medieval Sourcebook: Jewish Ethical Wills, 12th and 14th Centuries." <www.fordham.edu/halsall/source/jewish-wills.html> (March 4, 2000).

Miller, Sukie, with Suzanne Lipsett. *After Death: How People around the World Map the Journey after Life*. New York: Simon and Schuster, Touchstone, 1997.

Moskowitz, Faye. *A Leak in the Heart: Tales from a Woman's Life*. Boston: David R. Godine, 1985.

Muller, Wayne. *Sabbath: Restoring the Sacred Rhythm of Rest*. New York: Bantam, 1999.

Myss, Caroline. *Sacred Contracts*. New York: Crown, Harmony Books, 2001.

Needleman, Jacob. *Money and the Meaning of Life*. New York: Doubleday, 1991.

Norlander, Linda, and Kerstin McSteen. *Choices at the End of Life: Finding Out What Your Parents Want before It's Too Late*. Minneapolis: Fairview Press, 2001.

Norris, Kathleen. *Amazing Grace: A Vocabulary of Faith*. New York: Riverhead, 1998.

———. *The Cloister Walk*. New York: Riverhead, 1987.

Northrup, Christiane. *The Wisdom of Menopause: Creating Physical and Emotional Health and Healing During the Change.* New York: Bantam, 2003.

———. *Women's Bodies, Women's Wisdom: Creating Physical and Emotional Health and Healing.* New York: Bantam, 1994.

Nouwen, Henri J. M. *Life of the Beloved: Spiritual Living in a Secular World.* New York: Crossroad, 1992.

Orenstein, Debra, ed. *Lifecycles: Jewish Women on Life Passages and Personal Milestones.* Woodstock, Vt.: Jewish Lights, 1998.

Perlman, Debbie. *Flames to Heaven: New Psalms for Healing and Praise.* Wilmette, Ill.: RadPublishers, 1998.

Phillips, Michael, and Salli Rasberry. *The Seven Laws of Money.* New York: Random House, Word Wheel, 1974.

Piercy, Marge. *The Art of Blessing the Day.* New York: Alfred A. Knopf, 1999.

Pipher, Mary. *Another Country: Navigating the Emotional Terrain of Our Elders.* New York: Riverhead Books, 1999.

Pitzele, Peter. *Our Fathers' Wells.* San Francisco: HarperSanFrancisco, 1995.

———. *Scripture Windows.* Los Angeles: Torah Aura Productions, 1998.

Plaskow, Judith. *Standing Again at Sinai.* San Francisco: HarperSanFrancisco, 1991.

Plaskow, Judith, and Carol P. Christ, eds. *Weaving the Visions: New Patterns in Feminist Spirituality.* San Francisco: HarperSanFrancisco, 1989.

Pogrebin, Letty Cottin. *Getting Over Getting Older: An Intimate Journey.* Boston: Little, Brown and Company, 1996.

Prager, Marcia. *The Path of Blessing: Experiencing the Energy and Abundance of the Divine.* New York: Crown Publishers, Bell Tower, 1998.

Reich, Walter. *Hidden History of the Kovno Ghetto.* Boston: Little, Brown and Company, 1997.

Reimer, Gail Twersky, and Judith A. Kates. *Beginning Anew: A Woman's Companion to the High Holy Days.* New York: Simon and Schuster, 1997.

Reimer, Jack, and Nathaniel Stampfer, eds. *So That Your Values Live On: Ethical Wills and How to Prepare Them.* Woodstock, Vt.: Jewish Lights, 1991.

Remen, Rachel Naomi. *Kitchen Table Wisdom.* New York: Riverhead Books, 1996.

———. *My Grandfather's Blessings.* New York: Riverhead Books, 2000.

Rich, Adrienne. *On Lies, Secrets, and Silence.* New York: W. W. Norton and Company, 1979.

Roberts, Elizabeth, and Elias Amidon, eds. *Earth Prayers from around the World.* San Francisco: HarperSanFrancisco, 1991.

Robinson, Nancy A., ed. *Touched by Adoption.* Santa Barbara, Calif.: Green River Press, 1999.

Rogers, Natalie. *Emerging Woman: A Decade of Midlife Transitions.* Point Reyes, Calif.: Personal Press, 1980.

Roiphe, Anne. *Generation without Memory.* New York: Simon and Schuster, Linden Press, 1981.

———. *The Pursuit of Happiness.* New York: Summit Books, 1991.

Sarton, May. *Journal of a Solitude.* New York: W. W. Norton, 1973.

———. *Kinds of Love.* New York: W. W. Norton, 1970.

Schachter-Shalomi, Zalman. *Age-ing to Sage-ing: A Profound New Vision of Growing Older.* New York: Warner Books, 1997.

Schnur, Susan. "Beyond Forgiveness: Women, Can We Emancipate Ourselves from a Model Meant for Men?" *Lilith* (Fall 2001).

Scott-Maxwell, Florida. *The Measure of My Days.* New York: Penguin Books, 1979.

Sebold, Alice. *The Lovely Bones.* Boston: Little, Brown and Company, 2002.

Seixas, Abby. "Images of God: A Developmental Perspective." *Readings in Psychosynthesis: Theory, Process, and Practice.* Toronto, Ontario: The Department of Applied Psychology / The Ontario Institute for Studies in Education, 1985.

Sheehy, Gail. *New Passages: Mapping Your Life across Time.* New York: Random House, 1995.

————. *Passages.* New York: E. P. Dutton, 1976.

Sher, Gail. *One Continuous Mistake.* New York: Penguin, Arkana, 1999.

Shields, Carol. *The Stone Diaries.* New York: Penguin Books, 1994.

Siegal, Diana Laskin, Paula Brown Doress-Worters, and Wendy Sanford. *The New Ourselves Growing Older: Women Aging with Knowledge and Power.* New York: Touchstone Books, 1994.

Spangler, David. *Blessing: The Art and the Practice.* New York: Riverhead Books, 2001.

Spence, Linda. *Legacy: A Step-by-Step Guide to Writing Personal History.* Athens, Ohio: Ohio University Press, Swallow Press, 1997.

Steer, Diana. *Native American Women.* New York: Barnes and Noble Inc., 1996.

Steinberg, Sybil, ed. *Writing for Your Life #2.* Wainscott, New York: Pushcart Press, 1995.

Strassfeld, Sharon. *Everything I Know: Basic Life Rules from a Jewish Mother.* New York: Scribner, 1998.

Tana, Patti. *Ask the Dreamer Where Night Begins.* Dubuque, Iowa: Kendall/Hunt Publishing, 1986.

Tanakh: The Holy Scriptures. Philadelphia: The Jewish Publication Society, 1985.

Taylor, Daniel. *Letters to My Children: A Father Passes on His Values.* Downers Grove, Ill.: InterVarsity Press, 1989.

Tepper, Sheri S. *The Family Tree.* New York: Avon Books, 1997.

Tickle, Phyllis. *The Shaping of a Life: A Spiritual Landscape.* New York: Doubleday, 2001.

Ulrich, Laurel Thatcher. *The Age of Homespun: Objects and Stories in the Creation of an American Myth.* New York: Alfred A. Knopf, 2001.

———. *A Midwife's Tale: The Life of Martha Ballard, Based on Her Diary, 1785–1812.* New York: Vintage Books, 1990.

Umansky, Ellen M., and Dianne Ashton, eds. *Four Centuries of Jewish Women's Spirituality: A Sourcebook.* Boston: Beacon Press, 1992.

Viorst, Judith. *Necessary Losses.* New York: Simon and Schuster, 1986.

Wakefield, Dan. *The Story of Your Life: Writing a Spiritual Autobiography.* Boston: Beacon Press, 1990.

Walker, Alice. *Anything We Love Can Be Saved: A Writer's Activism: Essays, Speeches, Statements and Letters.* New York: Random House, 1997.

———. *In Search of Our Mothers' Gardens.* New York: Harvest, 1979.

———. *Possessing the Secret of Joy.* New York: Pocket Books, 1993.

———. *Sent by Earth: A Message from the Grandmother Spirit.* New York: Seven Stories Press, 2001.

Walker, Robert James. *Bridges of Madison County.* New York: Warner Books, 1997.

Waskow, Arthur. *Down-to-Earth Judaism: Food, Money, Sex, and the Rest of Life.* New York: William Morrow and Company, 1995.

Weil, Simone, et al. *The Need for Roots: Prelude to a Declaration of Duties Towards Mankind.* New York: Harper Colophon Books, 1971.

Weintraub, Simkha. *Healing of Soul, Healing of Body.* Woodstock, Vt.: Jewish Lights Publishing, 1994.

Wiesel, Elie. *All Rivers Run to the Sea.* New York: Schocken Books, 1995.

Wiesel, Marion, ed. *To Give Them Light: The Legacy of Roman Vishniac.* New York: Simon and Schuster, 1993.

Williamson, Marianne. *Everyday Grace: Having Hope, Finding Forgiveness, and Making Miracles.* New York: Riverhead Books, 2002.

———. *Illuminata: A Return to Prayer.* New York: Riverhead Books, 1994.

———. *A Return to Love: Reflections on the Principles of "A Course in Miracles."* New York: HarperCollins, 1996.

———. *A Woman's Worth.* New York: Ballantine Books, 1994.

Woolf, Virginia. *A Room of One's Own.* New York: Harvest, 1929.

Ywahoo, Dhyani. *Voices of Our Ancestors: Cherokee Teachings from the Wisdom Fire.* Boston: Shambhala, 1987.

Zborowski, Mark, and Elizabeth Herzog. *Life Is with People: The Culture of the Shtetl.* New York: Schocken Books, 1995.

Zornberg, Avivah Gottlieb. *The Beginning of Desire: Reflections on Genesis.* New York: Doubleday, 1995.

The Women's Legacies Foundation

A portion of the proceeds from this book will be used by The Women's Legacies Foundation to empower women with limited means to transform their unique and communal histories, stories, experiences, values, and wisdom into legacies for their families and communities. For more information, visit www.womenslegacies.com. There you can make a financial gift, read excerpts from women's spiritual-ethical wills, and exchange ideas about legacy writing with other women.

Women's Legacies Programs

Rachael Freed is available to facilitate retreats, programs, and legacy circles for groups, organizations, and faith communities. For more information call 612-558-3331 or email info@womenslegacies.com.

Facilitating Legacy Circles

For *The Legacy Circle Facilitator's Guide* or information about becoming a legacy circle facilitator, write to Women's Legacies, P.O. Box 16202, Minneapolis, Minnesota 55416; call 612-558-3331; or email info@womenslegacies.com.